JESUS IN THE MARGINS

JESUS IN THE MARGINS

RICK MCKINLEY

Multnomah® Publishers *Sisters, Oregon*

JESUS IN THE MARGINS
published by Multnomah Publishers, Inc.

© 2005 by Rick McKinley
International Standard Book Number: 1-59052-387-3

Cover illustration by Anneli Holmgren

Scripture quotations are from:
The Holy Bible, New International Version © 1973, 1984
by International Bible Society,
used by permission of Zondervan Publishing House.

Multnomah is a trademark of Multnomah Publishers, Inc.,
and is registered in the U.S. Patent and Trademark Office.
The colophon is a trademark of Multnomah Publishers, Inc.

Printed in the United States of America

For information:
MULTNOMAH PUBLISHERS, INC.
POST OFFICE BOX 1720
SISTERS, OREGON 97759

Library of Congress Cataloging-in-Publication Data

McKinley, Rick.
    Jesus in the margins / Rick McKinley.
        p. cm.
    ISBN 1-59052-387-3
    1. Christian life. 2. Marginality, Social—Religious aspects—
Christianity. I. Title.
    BV4509.5.M347 2005
    248.4—dc22

                                            2004022661

05 06 07 08 09 10—10 9 8 7 6 5 4 3 2 1 0

This book is dedicated to two great friends who made a huge difference in my life. Both went to heaven during the writing of this book. They were only in their fifties, but their impact on others was more than most would make in several lifetimes.

To Diane Lindstrom, a mentor, friend, and spiritual mom to so many. Your faith lives on in the lives of those you embraced. Thanks for showing me what courageous faith looks like and for loving me like Jesus.

To Scott Mitchell, thanks for calling me out of the margins and for being there for the good, the bad, and the ugly of my soul. Your strong compassion and love for Jesus overflowed to more people than you will ever know.
I miss you both, but I look forward to catching up over a glass of new wine.

CONTENTS

POSTCARDS FROM THE JOURNEY

Margins are those clear spaces along the edge of this page that keep the words from spilling off. Every book has them. You might jot notes in the margins, but for the most part they go unnoticed. They don't represent the book, and they don't define its message. They're simply there.

Society—our world, our culture—has margins just like this page does. They're places occupied by people who go unnoticed, misfits who seldom figure in when the mainline world defines and esteems itself. But they're there.

The margins are where I find people like me.

So many times it seems the rest of the world has gone ahead of me. They've created a mainstream life that mostly flows onward without me. Whether in church or in business or in relationships, there are times when I simply feel the rest of the world is out on the field playing, but it's a game I can't relate to. A game I'm not good at. A game I couldn't win.

So I stay in the margins. It's a place of security. It's where I find comfort.

THE AUTHOR, AGE 35

I've felt many times that I'm not very good at being a Christ-follower. There are issues, I guess, that make me feel isolated. For me, being loved is an awkward deal. I don't like having people care for me. I know that sounds weird because deep down we all want that. When someone does reach out to me, though, I tend to want to run. Some people would call it a fear of intimacy. Perhaps that's a good descriptive term, but it doesn't fix anything.

There's an illusion of safety in isolation. I won't be known there. If I'm not known, I can't be rejected. That's the unspoken mantra I've spent so many years abiding by. So I go to the margins. There's a kind of agreement there, an unwritten rule that everyone abides by: You get to be left alone. And even though there's this muffled scream coming from inside my heart, yelling out to people: *I'm dying in here!*

I find comfort in the fact that no one can hear that scream.

God? Well, he doesn't put up with my "fear of intimacy" too well. He invades my heart and screams back that he's here with me. It hasn't always been that way; in fact, most of my life, it's been just the opposite. Yeah, God keeps hounding me with his love and invitations.

The challenge that's always in front of me is to let him in.

I'm not alone here. The margins are crowded with people poured from the same mold. In many ways we share the same background, the same hurts, the same joys and hopes. So we share this same space—the margins.

Here are some postcards from their journeys…

Tiffany, Age 31

I don't usually tell anybody these kinds of things. I don't like being vulnerable. I'm seeing a counselor right now. I guess that's no big deal; so many people see counselors. It just makes me feel like I'm not normal, you know? Like something is wrong with me.

When I was nine years old, I was molested by a family member. At the time I really didn't understand what was happening, but I knew it wasn't normal. I was too scared to tell anyone, and because he was a family member, I felt that somehow my mom and dad allowed it to happen. Looking back, I can see that wasn't true, but at the time I didn't know any better.

The abuse continued until I was twelve and I told my mom what was happening. She cried so loud and for so long. I realized then the gravity of what had happened to me. The family member was confronted by my dad, and I've never seen him since, but we weren't a family that really dealt with problems thoroughly.

I was so relieved it was finally over that I just sort of tucked the whole thing into the back of my head and tried to forget it ever happened. Now that I'm older I realize I can't do that. I've never been able to scrub the sick feeling off my soul that was put there through the abuse. So I just go through life feeling that if anyone ever knew who I was on the inside, they would simply reject me. That's a crappy way to go through life, I know, but I don't know how else to feel.

I hate men. That's maybe a little strong. But every relationship I've ever had has been shallow because of it. I can't give myself to them, not emotionally anyway. I can have a sexual relationship but that's about as far as it goes. For some reason, trusting men with my body isn't a big deal; I just can't trust them with my heart.

I don't want to be single forever, but I don't seem to be able to get past it. I think it may all stem from the fact that I hate myself. I know that sounds harsh, but I've thought about it. I just don't like me. I have friends, but there's still a sense that I haven't really let them know me and my whole story. You have to have some pretty thick skin on your heart to live in my soap opera.

God? Well, I'm kind of angry with God. Why did he let it happen to me? He couldn't really love me. That's what I think. And I don't think God has much to say of any real significance.

I do hope—not a lot, but I do. I hope one day I can be honest with someone about my life and about what has happened to me, even the things I've done. And I hope that person can love me anyway.

David, Age 24

I'm still in college. It's my fourth college, and I've changed my major about a hundred times. I know. What a loser, right?

I see friends moving on to careers and becoming successful. The American dream. But I'm still here, lagging behind the rest of the pack, not even sure I want to catch up. I work just like they work. I just don't make as much money. I serve coffee at a franchise of the ever-present, ever-famous corporate coffee vendor from the Great Northwest.

The truth is, I don't think I'm even gonna stay in school. What's the point? For the most part, even my friends who have graduated are still working simple jobs.

I never knew my dad. He left when I was around three. My mom told me he was living in another state, but I've never tried to get in touch with him. I don't really care, I guess. I know this has affected me somehow, but I just kind of avoid thinking about it. My mom was great—she did all she could to fill his shoes. I just kind of wish I had that man in my life to prepare me for this whole deal of growing up.

You grow up with all this pressure to succeed, and you think, Yeah, yeah, yeah, I'll get it together one day. Then you wake up and you're twenty-four, still having to live with a bunch of people to make rent. Seems like life is passing me by.

I'm educated beyond my potential. I've taken philosophy, which taught me that life is meaningful only if you create meaning for yourself. I've taken biology, which taught me that I evolved by chance out of the primordial pond. I've taken business courses, which assumed my goal in life was to make money, a mistaken presupposition for this coffee bistro. All of them led to my collective pile of knowledge, and none of them connect into a meaningful whole. Not once in all my education has anyone asked the question, Why are you here? That would have been a great class, had I possessed the fortitude not to drop out of it.

Why am I here? I guess that's the question I'm waiting for someone to answer. I don't want to create my own existential reality. That would only be kidding myself. Who am I to create my own meaning? I can hardly get to work on time. If I ever buy into the fact that I'm here by evolutionary chance alone, I'm afraid I'll just "off" myself one day. I mean, what's the point?

But alas, if I join the rat race and buy into accumulation of cash as the meaning of life, I would simply die inside. I can't wake up, kiss my little blond wife on the cheek, climb into a Lexus, and drive off to throw elbows in the corporate boxing ring. I want something that's true and can speak to the growing emptiness that world seems to think I don't notice. (Tricky, aren't they?)

It's not that I'm in the worst place to be. I just can't get through a day without someone asking me what I want to be when I get done with school. That question pushes me into this loneliness where I feel like I'm huddled in a glass box that's only big enough for me. <u>I guess I just wish I was something, so I didn't have to become something.</u>

Jennifer, Age 29

I grew up homeless. Not on the streets or anything like that. I just didn't personally know the same meaning of "home" that I saw on TV.

My mom and dad got divorced when I was in fourth grade. I know divorce is no big deal anymore, but for some reason it still is a big deal to me. I guess that when I was kid, home made me feel okay. It was the place I could come to when I had a fight with my friends or when kids made fun of me at school, and then everything would be okay. I was safe again. The world out there was scary and mean at times, but home was the place where everything would be okay. It was a haven to protect you. It was peace.

Then one day all that was gone. My dad moved into our house with some lady who would become my "stepmom," and Mom and I moved out and into an apartment. I had to change schools, and I only saw Dad a couple of times a month. All of a sudden, at nine years old, I felt like all the scary stuff in the world had come crashing through the windows of my house like a hurricane. Mom and I were walking around with shards of glass sticking out of our hearts, and Dad was missing.

It probably took until I was in high school to get used to it. I know everyone's parents get divorced, and I'm supposed to get over it. But I've had a tough time doing that. I remember crying a lot at night, wanting it all to go back to normal. I so missed Dad and Mom being together.

I thought the divorce was my fault for a long time. I think I kind of still do. If I could have kept them together, I could have kept my world from crashing down. Before the divorce, home had been the one thing in the world that seemed right, but all that goodness turned out to be an illusion. It wasn't real.

Now I don't think home can really exist. It can't be a real thing, at least for most people. And that's so sad.

And God seems about as far away to me as those warm holidays at home before the divorce. I don't see God as really relevant to me. I want the safety of life in that illusion of home, not some religious answer for it. I don't want the sterile hallways of a church. I want to go back home. Listen to me—I sound like a Kodak commercial. That's how I feel, though. I don't tell a lot of people about it, but it's true. I still feel homeless.

Peter, Age 55

I'm pretty successful. I've made a lot of money and I have lots of things. Don't get me wrong, I'm no Bill Gates. But I live pretty comfortably.

My kids, Tim and Melissa, are out of the house now. Tim is in college and Melissa graduated last year and is engaged. I wish I were tighter with my kids. I wasn't around that much when they were growing up—I had to travel and we ended up moving a lot with the company. I always wanted to give them the stuff I never had, you know? Working was my way of loving them.

My wife, Linda, and I just moved into a new home. It's the best house we've ever owned. It's on a golf course, and it gives me an excuse to play in my backyard. Lately, though, I've been thinking a lot at night. I can't seem to sleep, so

I've started asking these questions. They're questions that have popped into my mind from time to time, but I always pushed them back into their hole. They're questions that critique everything I've been about for the last thirty years.

Why don't your kids like you?

Who do you really know that you could call a friend?

If all your toys get taken away, who are you?

I hate these questions. I just can't seem to make them go away. I don't have answers for them. I have all this stuff, but what I don't have is relationships. Not ones that are deep, anyway.

Sometimes at night I lay there and my whole life feels like I just opened all the presents at Christmas and now I'm bored and lonely again.

I feel guilty for not being there for my kids. I also feel a bit ripped off. I feel ripped off that all the things I thought were important have ended up stealing the things that were most important. Now I sit here and wonder who the hell I am.

All the other guys at work don't really struggle with this. At least, it doesn't seem that way. They hold a confidence that I've somehow lost. I had it in my thirties and forties, but I seem to have misplaced it over the last few years. The security I was looking for is still there—I have my investments, my 401(k), and pretty good health. But I still feel insecure about life.

I just don't have any answers. I think I may be afraid to admit that everything I've been about is wrong.

Liz, Age 27

I grew up in a great home. I had two great parents who loved me. We went to church as long as I can remember, and my father was a deacon there. When I was seven, I remember having a very real encounter with God. The preacher was preaching and I don't even remember now what he was talking about, but I remember feeling touched by God deep in my heart. I went forward at the end of the service and asked God to forgive me and enter my life. From that day forward, I've had a relationship with God.

Growing up in the church was a different kind of growing up. I never really understood where I fit in the church. When we came through the doors, I would be rushed off to a class with people who were my age. I went from class to class as I grew up, all the while wondering when I would get to be in the real church. I felt kind of like God's kid who needed babysitting while God did his real business with adults who could understand him better. We learned all the stories of the Bible, but didn't talk much about how it was all supposed to fit into our lives.

As I got older and went to high school, I

remember the focus changing quite a bit. <u>The lessons began to be about protecting us from the world around us.</u> I had friends in high school who didn't go to church, yet they were my best friends. For some reason this was wrong. We were often taught that if we wanted to follow God, we would need to choose to leave the friends we had because they would bring us down.

It seemed that somewhere along the way God quit liking nonreligious people. The only way I could really live for God was by living my life in a religious world and not in the world where everyone else lived. The problem was, I really liked these people. They were my friends. The only way to solve the problem seemed to be to create a little compartment in my head where I could keep my God stuff. I could bring it out on Sundays or when I was with religious people, then the rest of the time I could just live my life.

I guess it made me feel like I was in no-man's-land a lot, loving God but not fitting into the religious world. Loving people in the real world, but feeling I shouldn't hang out with them. I was an alien in both worlds.

I've gotten older and I've married, and I now have two kids. I live my life pretty much in the religious world. We're in a great church and our kids go to a Christian school we love. I don't really have any friends anymore who don't believe in God, so I guess I've crossed over. I feel like it's not right though. I feel like I should have relationships with people who are different. It's been so long now since I lived in that world. I don't think I would even know where to start making friends with people like that.

My relationship with God is still there. At times I feel like I'm going through the motions. I just can't make it all connect. It's like I have to do one or the other. It's a weird place to be.

I think I may be the only person who struggles with this. At church everyone seems so happy, like they never want to know what's happening in the real world. I do, though. I want to love God and the people around me in the world who don't understand God yet. But that feels wrong. Or maybe it's just me.

HONESTY

These are the dwellers of the margins. People just like me. Yes, it's a crowded place, for sure. But it's not like we wake up every day and stare these realities in the face. They don't always flash like neon signs in our brains. Many times the realities of our brokenness operate beneath the surface of the soul and quietly gnaw at our hearts. They subtly whisper to us that something inside us is a little off, so we move to the margins to be with others who share our painful journey.

And in those places in the margins we hold out the silent hope that one day we will be loved. That we'll be known for who we are, and when we put all our stuff on the table—everything that has happened to us, all the mistakes we've made, every bad thing we've done—that someone will look at all of it and say, "I love you. I accept you as you are."

When we bump into each other in the crowded margins, we doubt we will ever hear those words. And we admit it.

The great thing about the margins is the honesty.

No one here is still playing games.

We're all ready to have an authentic look at life. We desperately want love and acceptance, but we just can't bring ourselves to sacrifice honesty in order to get it.

But there is someone in whom I find incredible hope. His life has so many parallels to ours, so many marginal characteristics—while at the same time, he offers significant answers to a lot of our questions. I believe if we give an honest look at who this man is, and listen afresh to the honest responses he always gives, we just might find some answers to our deepest longings.

Meanwhile, I try never to feel bad about living in the margins. They may, in fact, be the true birthplace of real life.

JESUS THE ILLEGITIMATE CHILD

When we pull back the curtain on his life, we discover that Jesus knows what it's like to be marginalized. He knows what it's like to have society shove you to the side of the page, to not really be accepted, and in the end, to be totally rejected. He can identify with life in the margins, because when God came down to earth in the person of Jesus Christ, the margins is where he landed. On purpose.

IF I WERE GOD

If I were the Son of God coming to earth, I'm sure I'd choose to do it in spectacular fashion. I would probably come down on the middle of the field at the Super Bowl, like those guys who parachute in during the halftime show. You're on high-definition TV and the whole world is watching. All the lights go out in the stadium, except for spotlights swirling around wildly in every direction, and the announcer declares in his dramatic baritone, "Ladies and gentlemen, the moment you've been waiting for…"

Suddenly, the spotlights aim upward in unison toward a single point high in the night sky. And then I impressively, slowly descend unaided from the sky. And the announcer shouts, "Yes! The Savior of the world, the Alpha and Omega, Creator of the universe, God in the flesh! Please give a life-changing welcome to…

"JEEESUUUUS!"

At this point the stadium crowd goes nuts. The cameras zoom in for a close-up, and my dazzling image floods the massive Jumbotron, not to mention the TV screens in hundreds of millions of homes worldwide. Everyone would know I've come. No one could possibly miss the fact that God was in town. They would realize I was here to save the world and that they'd better pay attention to what I have to say.

That's how I'd do it.

For some reason, God did it very differently.

WHEN THE LORD CAME TO TOWN

Jesus showed up in a rural town called Nazareth. Not much of a place, really. There were probably ten, maybe fifteen thousand people living there, and they were a less-cultivated class—more like blue-collar or hillbilly types, rude and crude. Years later, a

guy named Nathanael became a disciple of Jesus,
but when he first heard about the man and where
he had come from, Nathanael's first response was,
"Nazareth! Can anything good come from there?"
(John 1:46). In that day, by most people's thinking,
you could hardly be of any consequence if you grew
up in Nazareth, even if you were a good religious
person. The town's name carried a stigma.

I lived for a number of years in a small town in
eastern Oregon about the same size as Nazareth. After
growing up in big cities, moving there meant a radical
shift for me. I discovered that in a place that small,
gossip spreads like wildfire. Everybody knows everybody's business, and you can't maintain the kind of
anonymity you have in big cities.

In the town where I lived, the local newspaper was
delivered every afternoon. It wasn't a big paper; I once
folded up the whole thing and put it in my wallet.
And it didn't have much to report, since in a small
town there isn't always a lot going on. But people read
it as eagerly as if it was the *World Headline News* and
we were in the middle of the most decisive battle in a
Great War.

The part of the paper everyone turned to first was
called the Record. The Record noted any kind of
criminal activity that had taken place in the town.
Now this town wasn't known for major crimes; that
wasn't what you found in the Record. What showed
up there were the names of the people who had done

some kind of mischievous thing and gotten busted for it.

I was working with high school students at the time, and one day the names of some of them showed up in the Record for getting MIPs (a ticket for being a Minor in Possession). The cops had busted a party and found these sixteen-year-old kids there with beers in their hands.

The next morning, when I walked into the office where I worked, I discovered that everyone there knew about these certain individuals. In the grocery store, in the coffee shop, everyone was talking about them.

Later I met with these kids and they were very much aware they'd done something wrong. What was more mortifying than anything was that the whole town knew who they were and what they had done. They had become notorious. Walking around town, people would avoid making eye contact with them, then stare at them from a distance.

That's just the kind of setting Jesus arrives in.

And to make matters worse, in his case, there is gossip of the ugliest kind surrounding him from the start.

MESSY AND MYSTERIOUS

Rather than appearing as the fabulous halftime performer on Super Bowl Sunday, Jesus comes into the world as an infant, the weakest of the weak, com-

pletely unnoticed by most of the outside world.
What's more, he shows up in the womb of an
unwed teenage mom. The story has scandal written
all over it.

Mary, his mom, was probably somewhere between
twelve and fifteen years old when she conceived Jesus.
She's a young teenager who is engaged to a man
(somewhat older, probably) whose name is Joseph.
He's a carpenter, another of Nazareth's blue-collar
folks. And since everybody knows everything in small
towns, all of Nazareth knows that Joseph and Mary
are engaged.

Then comes the shocking news. When Joseph dis-
covers Mary is pregnant, he's a broken man. All the
things run through his mind that would run through
anyone's mind if he found out the young woman he
loves and is engaged to is carrying a child, even
though he's never had sex with her. Joseph decides to
break off their relationship quietly, trying to make the
whole horrible mess go away without totally destroy-
ing Mary's reputation, when the angel of God shows
up and explains to him what God is up to. The angel
tells Joseph that the Holy Spirit has conceived the
child in Mary's womb, and the child will be the
world's Savior. Joseph immediately marries the young
teenage mom, whom he loves with all his heart. So
here's this young couple, caught up in the midst of the
most radical, mysterious plan of God there ever was.

Nevertheless, the whole town of Nazareth is

gossiping, whispering behind Mary's back and her swollen belly. *Is that Joseph's baby conceived out of wedlock? Or has Mary had a fling with another man?* And though Mary and Joseph are mercifully far away in Bethlehem when the birth occurs, they eventually move back to Nazareth to raise their family. And in everyone's way of thinking, this little boy who's come back with them is indeed illegitimate.

He's stuck with a label.

HE CAME TO STAY

What a strange context for the coming of Jesus to earth, that God would take on such scorn and scandal by showing up at the corner of No and Where, inviting rejection from a Jewish society that so decidedly frowned on anyone of illegitimate birth.

God doesn't give much weight to society's regard or cultural assumptions. He isn't afraid of what people might think. In his crazy purposes and plans, he comes to the scandalous margins of society in order to identify with those of us who live in those places.

That's where Jesus arrives. And more. He doesn't come to the margins just to rise up out of them, like some against-all-odds Rocky success story. No, he comes to the margins to stay there and live there and work there. That is the focus of his mission.

When Jesus is an adult, he goes public and starts

telling people who he is and what he's doing. One day he walks into the synagogue in Nazareth and opens up the scroll of the Scriptures to Isaiah chapter 61. To the townspeople of Nazareth—and ultimately to all the world—he reads out loud his life vision, his mission statement, his job description. In essence he's letting everyone know that his calling is, in fact, a mission to marginalized people.

Listen to what he says.

He says he's come *to preach good news to the poor,* to people who are broken economically, to those who don't have the resources it takes to make it in this world.

He says he's come *to bind up the brokenhearted,* those to whom life has been extremely cruel and tragic. Jesus has come to bandage those wounds.

He says he's come *to proclaim freedom for the captives and release from darkness for the prisoners,* those who have walked outside legal boundaries and been rejected by society. Whether they're emotionally imprisoned or physically imprisoned or both, Jesus is here to free them. To those who've lost hope, he will bring them out of that darkness and into light.

The rest of the Isaiah passage describes more of what Jesus has come to do:

> To comfort all who mourn, and provide for
> those who grieve in Zion—to bestow on them
> a crown of beauty instead of ashes, the oil of
> gladness instead of mourning, and a garment

of praise instead of a spirit of despair. They
will be called oaks of righteousness, a planting
of the LORD for the display of his splendor.

Here's the paradox: Society may have named you
"poor" or "brokenhearted" or "prisoner," but Jesus
says, "I'm going to do something radically different
in your life. Right there among the mess in the margins of this world, I am going to crown you with
beauty." Somehow in the midst of your grief and
your loss, he'll let this oil of gladness wash over you.
You'll be given hope. Joy and praise will break
through the clouds of heavy despair.

Yes, society names you, but there's *another* who
names you, someone whose perception of you is ultimately more powerful than anything society can label
you with. His name for you is something as stunning
as Oak of Righteousness, a Planting of the Lord for
the Display of His Splendor.

Which means, if you want to observe the glory of
the Lord, if you want to witness the display of his
splendor and his work, you have to go to the margins
to see it. Because it's in the margins where broken lives
get mended and prisoners get set free and the poor
hear good news. Jesus says that *they* are the display of
his splendor.

As Jesus was saying these things to the people of Nazareth, they were mumbling to themselves, *Who does this guy think he is? Isn't that trollop Mary his mother? Isn't this the guy who was born illegitimately?*

That label again.

The people grew furious with Jesus. He was so marginalized in their thinking that they were ready to kill him. They drove him out of town to the top of a cliff, intending to throw him off. But in the end he walked silently through the crowd and left them to themselves and their anger. It wasn't his time to die.

It was as if Jesus was telling them that day, "You have no power to name me. You tell me I'm illegitimate and unacceptable, but you need to know that the Spirit of the sovereign Lord is on me. The Father has anointed me to do these things, and you can't hold me back or keep me down."

God will not be mocked by the world around us. He overcomes it. He will not be labeled by our socioeconomic baggage. He is not banking his chips on making it big in this world. He has come to redeem the margins.

Jesus shows us how we are to find our identity, acceptance, and legitimacy from the Father. God is ultimately in control over anyone and everyone in society who would try to control and label us.

Jesus was able to trust that and so should we.

There's no doubt society possesses enormous power to name us and tell us who we are. To say whether we're good or bad. To pronounce us acceptable or rejected. To tell us if we're legitimate or illegitimate. It's so hard to go through life and not care about or be influenced by what people say and think, and their judgment stays with us. The labels stick.

Most of us have been subconsciously "named" by at least some of the negative experiences and circumstances in our past. And going through the world knowing you're one of the unlucky ones, one of the unlovely people, can be a traumatic experience. Surrounded by scandal, we live in fear that somehow even more of the things we've done, the bad things we've thought in the deep recesses of our heart, will someday show up on the Record for the whole world to read and know about. And we'll be marginalized for life.

In the margins we feel deeply our own illegitimacy. We feel strongly society's verdict that we aren't good enough, aren't acceptable enough, haven't performed enough. We may feel our illegitimacy economically—no matter how hard we work or try, it seems we never rise above the poverty level. Society decides how much money you need to make to be acceptable, but we sense that maybe we'll never rise above that line. Our illegitimacy may be felt in countless other ways, sometimes on several levels at once.

I live in Portland, Oregon, which reportedly has the largest number of street kids per capita in America. These kids have been told by society that they're throwaways, that they don't belong. That they'll never make enough money, never work hard enough, never be smart enough. The overwhelming weight of these names, placed on them by their families and society, pressures them into letting themselves be "pimped out"—that is, making money through sexual favors. They find themselves given over to drug addiction, because in Portland heroin is cheap and accessible. Violence is rampant and they find themselves clinging to one another, trying to find love or acceptance or the slightest glimmer of hope.

That's just one small part of the margins, just one of so many categories of people who feel illegitimate and who, in one way or another, sense that society sees them as unacceptable.

They're the people that Isaiah 61 says Jesus came to love—the poor, the broken, the needy. And when the love of Jesus is brought to a place like theirs, it shows up like a diamond on black velvet. It just sparkles brilliantly because it's so foreign to these people's existence.

The fact is, the most crucial piece of our real identity—the name that ultimately overrides all others—is who we are in God's eyes.

Love doesn't come to the poor or the broken in the margins with the purpose of effecting total escape from this life of brokenness. The love of Jesus doesn't come to make us fit into American culture; it's here to make us fit into heaven. His love is here to complete us.

Jesus isn't really concerned with moving us into a new economic strata or a different social structure, and I think the church has missed this. Jesus isn't so much concerned about removing you from the margins as he is with helping you understand that you don't have to be *named* by the margins of this society. He says you're named by God. Jesus himself was a carpenter, then a homeless wanderer, and he died the death of a criminal. But none of that named him. He knew he was the Father's Son.

His invitation to us is to walk away from the names placed on us by society and to hear and believe the new names the Father gives us.

Legitimate.

Accepted.

Loved.

Cared for.

Forgiven.

To hear and believe these names is to be given the oil of gladness to replace the spirit of despair.

The challenge before us is only to *believe*. Sounds simple. But we won't believe until we truly see who

Jesus is, until we identify with his rejection and get to know him in a fresh way. Not as some blond and blue-eyed cultural icon who comes around with a smile at Christmas and Easter to bless our lives and make us feel better. Or like a statue on a distant pedestal, where he's crowned with halos and surrounded by angels. That Jesus remains far removed from our hearts because we can't connect to a Savior who doesn't understand our life or know the nitty-gritty of the margins where we live.

No, we need to see Jesus as he really is: exactly in the way he presented himself. That's what we're here for in this book, and we have more to discover.

JESUS THE CHURCH MISFIT

It was a warm Sunday morning in California. I got up out of bed and felt that I needed to go to church. My fists were bloody from the night before, although I had no recollection of where I'd been or what I'd done. My bedroom was turned upside down—I remember thinking it looked the way my life was headed. I knew something needed to change, and a weird desire began to stir inside me.

A desire to find God.

WHY ARE YOU HERE?

My life up to that point had never really included church. My family went to church once when I was about nine years old. It was Easter and my mom talked us all into going. I remember sitting in a pew and singing hymns out of a book. My father was always something of a clown, and he began singing like an operatic tenor with full vibrato, and me, being all of nine, I was embarrassed to death, staring at the floor and giggling. As we walked out, the pastor was at the door shaking hands, and he complimented my father on his great voice. My dad smiled and thanked him and I almost wet myself, I was laughing so hard.

That was my entire experience with religion. I had never gone back to church and had no idea who Jesus was.

As a high school senior I was voted the person "most likely to die with a beer in his hand." I was a party animal and I went away to a party college, believing with all my heart that this was what my life needed to be about. The school I enrolled in was ranked number one for partying in *Playboy* magazine that year. Hey, I wasn't searching for the best academic institution; I was looking for a good time.

It wasn't everything I'd hoped it would be. After a few months in college, I began to sense this huge void that no amount of partying could fill. My life was empty of meaning. And I knew that if people knew *the real me* they probably wouldn't like me. As long as I was being the funny dude and the life of the party, I had plenty of friends. But if I wanted to talk about personal problems or my questions about life, my so-called friends stayed away in droves.

I finally dropped out of school. There had been good times, but in the end the experience only deepened my questions about life. I was left with more problems and fewer answers. Still, when I got home, I continued partying. The path became darker and more difficult, and I realized I was becoming addicted to drugs and alcohol.

When I woke up that Sunday with a desire to go to church, I chose the one closest to my house. It happened to be Palm Sunday, the week before Easter, commemorating the time Jesus rode on a donkey into Jerusalem to a celebratory welcome, only to be rejected and crucified in a matter of days. But I had no idea what Palm Sunday was about then.

I walked into a large church and sat down in the back. No one really talked to me. I felt like I'd walked into another world, another culture. The people all seemed happy, as though their lives were perfect. Mine, on the other hand, was a complete wreck. I couldn't identify or relate. I just wanted to hide in the corner.

In front of me was a group of high school students, many of whom had known me and my reputation. Some of them looked back at me, and they began to talk among themselves. I could sense they wondered what in the world I was doing there. Church was *their* thing, and maybe they thought I was intruding. Finally the group's ringleader, who knew me from our playing days on the football team, came back and sat down next to me.

He said, "We're just wondering why you're here today."

"I have no idea." Which was true.

He didn't say much more and went back to his group. I heard him tell them, "He doesn't know." Then they turned and faced the front and went on with their lives.

CAPTIVATED SOUL

The service began and I heard about this person of Jesus and his love for me. It really got my attention. I heard that his love for the world led him to a cross where he was executed, and that no matter what I'd done, good or bad, God loved me and was ready to forgive me. Divine justice demanded that God punish me for my sin, but instead of punishing me, he punished himself.

He killed his Son to pay for my sins.

That captivated my soul.

Could this hope fill the void of meaning in my life, the vast emptiness I'd been trying to fill up with so many other things? I didn't really care if any of these people liked me. I had already been popular in school, and I wasn't here for a popularity contest. I was simply trying to find God. And I was very determined to discover who he was.

Unfortunately, for countless other people, that wall of church culture is just too difficult to penetrate. I've talked to so many who truly, deeply wanted to discover Jesus. But they had looked at these well-dressed people rejecting them from the pews ahead of them and saw there a God who must also be ready to reject them. And so they completely blew off their search for Jesus.

The sad reality is that the church today many times separates people from the real Jesus, the Jesus who was marginalized by his culture and who walked in the same margins you and I walk in.

Part of the problem is that somewhere along the line, the church adopted a *consumer mentality*. They bought into the idea Rodney Clapp has called "church as a vendor of religious goods and services." They're selling Jesus. And the only way to really sell Jesus is to make people think the product works—that if you come and believe like they do, your life will become shiny and happy and perfect. So the church started thinking they had to protect Jesus. They created this Christian-life facade to advertise Jesus as an irresistible product that will make you over into a perfect person.

After years in the church, I began to see that underneath those shiny suits and happy smiles were people just like me who were broken and sinful and desperately in need of acceptance and love and forgiveness. But for the first ten years of following Jesus, I tried to fit in with this consumer church culture, and it just didn't work. I was still a marginalized kid. I was the redheaded cousin nobody wants to take credit for: I made it into the family, but only on a fluke.

In Jesus' time, the religious community didn't accept
him either. He didn't fit in. He lived in the margins.
Over the years I've found incredible comfort in this,
because I realize I'm not alone.

More and more people today believe that the
church as an institution is not an authentic or viable
way to connect with God. We want to go someplace
where people are straight-up about things and deal
with life in a real way. We're searching for a place
where everyone can admit who they are, let down
their guard, and confess that they, too, need a Savior.
The truth is, all of us who have a relationship with
God can do so only because:

1. God has forgiven us.
2. We're still desperately needy people.

One Sunday morning while I was speaking in
the faith community that I pastor, I noticed a man
walk into the church and sit down, a man I hadn't
seen before. He was in his late twenties and covered
with tattoos. He reminded me of myself when I
walked into church that Palm Sunday morning years
ago. He sat there and listened to my sermon, listened to the worship, and watched as we celebrated
communion to remember how Jesus loved us
enough to die in our place. I watched as he wept.
People talked with him and loved him, and he
began to understand for the first time that there is a

God who loves him, too, and his name is Jesus.

A few days later, this man sat in my office and asked to hear more about the story of Christ. I began explaining that God wanted to forgive—and could forgive—him for all he'd done in the past. He began to weep again. He then said something that struck me, words that showed me that he really understood deep down this love of God. His words took me back to when I was eighteen and felt this same hope for the first time. This man said to me, "I don't want to sound like an ass, but this is better than the days when my daughters were born."

Reminiscent of the pivotal moments when his daughters came into the world as gifts of life, he recognized the gift of eternal life and forgiveness from God the Father through the Son was the best news he had ever heard. This man was overwhelmed with the realization that God accepted him for who he really was. There was no stumbling block on his way to Jesus. He could be real and put all his stuff on the table, and Jesus would accept him. And there were people in this place who were ready to love him, too.

He had tried to find Jesus through the church over the years, but each time he did, he felt rejected by people. I assured him that when Jesus walked the earth, he was treated the same way by the religious establishment.

The very first miracle Jesus performs is at a wedding in a Galilean town called Cana. He's there with his friends as guests at a wedding reception for a young couple. Wedding parties could last for days back then, and halfway through this particular party, there's a problem. Mary, the mother of Jesus, comes to him and says, "They have no wine."

Now the bride or bridegroom would have experienced a tremendous sense of shame and embarrassment over this, because it probably meant they didn't have enough money to provide sufficient refreshment for the duration of the party. But Jesus has compassion on the young couple and does the impossible. We read about it in chapter 2 of the Gospel of John:

> Nearby stood six stone water jars, the kind used by the Jews for ceremonial washing, each holding from twenty to thirty gallons. Jesus said to the servants, "Fill the jars with water"; so they filled them to the brim.
>
> Then he told them, "Now draw some out and take it to the master of the banquet." They did so, and the master of the banquet tasted the water that had been turned into wine. He did not realize where it had come from, though the servants who had drawn the water knew. Then he called the bridegroom

aside and said, "Everyone brings out the choice wine first and then the cheaper wine after the guests have had too much to drink; but you have saved the best till now."

This, the first of his miraculous signs, Jesus performed at Cana in Galilee. He thus revealed his glory, and his disciples put their faith in him.

What's stunning to me in all this is that Jesus does a miracle which, if he did it today, would cause the religious community to seriously question his propriety. He makes one hundred and eighty gallons of wine for people who are already a little more than half lit. But the Bible says that in doing this he reveals his glory and wins his disciples' faith.

When I was in Bible college, I was assigned to write a few different papers that tried to prove the wine Jesus made wasn't alcoholic. It was as though they didn't want Jesus to be who he really is.

Like they wanted to cover up what Jesus did.

They wanted us to say he had made the best grape juice you ever tasted. But I've had wine and I've had grape juice, and I know that if someone gave me a cup of grape juice I would never respond, "This is the best wine I've ever tasted!"

The church wants to protect Jesus' image rather than proclaim the real and living Christ. We want to protect him from the appearance of doing things that wouldn't fit into today's church culture.

Soon after changing the water into wine, Jesus goes to the temple in Jerusalem and, angered by what he sees there, makes a big rope of cords. He starts cracking this whip as he thunders through the temple, overturning vendors' tables and setting free the sacrificial animals for sale. He shouts, "Take these things away! How dare you turn my Father's house into a market!"

The temple courtyard had become a strip mall where people were required to buy religious goods and services in order to worship God. The priests had created a *wall*, a barrier that kept people from knowing who God truly was and how he wanted to love them.

The religious leaders freaked out when Jesus started messing up their building. They came to him and demanded, "Who do you think you are? What right do you have to tear up our temple and tell us our worship is wrong?"

Jesus would later be labeled by this same religious community as a glutton and a drunkard, just because he hung out with marginalized people and had the nerve to eat and drink with them. But he was willing to be marginalized by the religious community because he so passionately cared about the average person in great need, the person who isn't always smiling and happy and wearing the best clothes. Jesus came here to love the people in the margins and, ultimately, to transform the religious community that created the barriers that kept the average person from finding God.

FRIEND OF SINNERS

One day, Jesus comes across a tax collector named Levi. This is a time and place where Jewish tax collectors are hated by society and, in particular, by the religious community because they collect taxes from their own people on behalf of the reviled Roman rulers. And it is common practice for the tax men to charge too much and pocket a little extra cash for themselves.

Levi is a tax collector, which means he has a hard heart and thick skin. In his job, you can't really care about people and their circumstances. Levi has heard every excuse and every sob story for why people can't pay their taxes. They tell him they're out of work or their child is dying or their house and crops have been destroyed, but Levi doesn't care. He just wants their money.

In high school, I had a football coach who was a "repo man." His job was to repossess cars from people who weren't paying their bills. One time he asked me to go with him. We went up to this house and knocked, and the door opened. My coach stepped forward, threw the man of the house against the wall, and demanded the car keys. He got them and we left. As I drove away in the car that we had just repossessed, I wondered what must be going on in the coach's heart that he would be so hardened as to not even ask this guy why he was unable to pay his bill. My coach didn't care; he was just doing his job. That's sort of how I picture Levi's heart.

Then one day Jesus walks by and says, "Levi, come follow me." Out of all the crowd on the busy street that day, Jesus picks out the most irreligious, hard-hearted individual you would ever hope to meet. Jesus asks him to drop everything he's doing and become one of his closest friends and followers.

So Levi gets up from the collection table and walks away from his job. He has never been treated with such respect and acceptance by a religious person. He is used to being rejected by them. If Levi had ever wondered about God, he probably assumed that God simply didn't like him, if only because the people who claimed to be closest to God didn't like him.

The first thing Levi does is throw a party for Jesus.

Not being a real religious guy, he probably doesn't know all the rules—such as, *You don't throw huge keggers for rabbis.* But Levi did just that. And he invites all his friends to come and meet this incredible man.

Jesus goes to the party, breaking yet another religious rule, but he doesn't care. He's always interested in the Levis of the world who are ignorant enough to throw a kegger for God. That's who Jesus has come to love.

While he's at the party, the religious people are outside, staking out the joint like cops waiting to bust Jesus for being out past curfew. They're asking his disciples, "What's wrong with him? Why is he eating and drinking with such people? Why is he a friend of sinners?"

I think that phrase right there is the most perfect way to explain Jesus: He's a friend of sinners. He's there in the margins with the average Joe, with people whose lives are broken and tattered and sinful. People who have had horrible things happen to them and done horrible things back. Jesus is in there accepting them and tolerating their behavior. Why? Because he wants them to know that he loves them.

These aren't people who would get up early and go to church, or figure out how to jump through all of the ritualistic hoops thrown up by the religious community. These people have written off all that. They sleep in on Sundays and watch football and go to the mall. They're just the average person on the street.

Jesus is a friend to people like that, which prevents him from fitting in with the moral lifestyle of religious people. And so he's marginalized by them. They reject him.

WHAT GOD THINKS

Every time I read these stories about Jesus I am filled with incredible hope, because I'm the kind of guy who would much more likely have been found at Levi's party than at the synagogue. And Jesus went there after me.

One of the mistakes often made by those of us in the margins is we assume that if churchgoers don't like us, then God must not like us.

Through years of Bible college and working in churches, I remember always really wanting to go out and love those people who would never walk through the church doors. People who have given up trying to be a religious person—they realize they can't play the game well enough and have no interest in putting on a facade. These are the people Jesus wants his people to go be with and love.

If you feel that God doesn't like you and thinks you're not good enough for him, then somewhere along the way someone caused you to think that. The beautiful news is, this is *not* how God sees you or thinks about you. God knows you need help and hope, that you have sin that needs to be forgiven. But he also knows you have a huge capacity for love, to understand his love for you.

He longs to show you an untainted picture of what his love looks like. That you would see this man Jesus for who he truly is: a person who was marginalized by the religious community—but only because of his genuine love.

REDEMPTION:
SO WHAT?

One of our family vacations was to Cabo San Lucas in Baja California, where palm trees sway in a continuous gentle breeze. There the ocean waves crash so hard against the shoreline you can feel the sand shake on the beach. The night sky is amazing, countless stars blazing through the darkness and reflected on the water. For ten days I was living the good life in paradise.

It was in paradise that an unsettling thought scurried through my mind: *Do I really need Jesus?* I imagined all sorts of ways I could move to a place like this, and I believed that if this were my daily experience I would have no worries. After all, the saying in Cabo goes, "No bad days." I spoke with other Americans who had moved to the area, and they seemed to be enjoying a worry-free existence.

Life in paradise.

The life I wanted.

But then there were the thousands of people living in incredible poverty all around me, large extended families crammed into one-bedroom houses. I didn't want to think about them, though. I was living the good life.

When we step back and recognize that we have defined "the good life" as something we can obtain by ourselves *for* ourselves, we begin to see the absurdity of redemption. Jesus came to redeem us from something *we* don't think is a problem. Why should he die on the cross for me? I'm living the good life.

And so the question becomes, *So what?*

CAN I GET MY DEPOSIT BACK?

At this point you may get the impression that Jesus just came to identify with those of us who live in the margins. He does identify with us, but that's not the big idea of why he came. He came to redeem us from our sin.

But the word *redemption* doesn't hold much meaning in the world I live in. We bring back our bottles and cans to the store and redeem our deposit. Depending where you live, you may get a dime or a nickel or next to nothing. Other than that, the word *redemption* does not hold a lot of meaning for most of us.

Redemption is a theological word that means "the purchase back of something that had been lost, by the payment of a ransom." Jesus was on a mission to purchase back those who were lost. To get them back for his Father. Jesus is still on that mission.

The Bible speaks of Jesus as purchasing us back to God by dying in our place. In saying this, there are some general assumptions being made, the first being that something is keeping us from being fully his to begin with. That something is sin, brokenness, the stuff that keeps us in the margins. The second assumption is that God is *giving* us something. That something is his life in us. Over and over in Scripture God calls us to reimagine what life could be if we lived it in him, with his life in us.

PENDULUM SWING

We look at Jesus and we often picture God as a merciful lover. God is also just and righteous, but if we're being honest, most of us would say we prefer to just think of God as merciful and loving. We tend to disconnect with the idea of a holy God who is full of wrath toward sin. But the Bible leaves us with a tension between the two images. We never have one without the other, and we must come to grips with this tension, no matter how uncomfortable it feels.

When the tension is released—when we refuse to see God for who he truly is—the pendulum swings toward one side or the other. On the one side we have a soft and cuddly Jesus, a grandfatherly God who chuckles at our antics but doesn't really care what we do. He is a dysfunctional parent robbed of any authority and power. He is "buddy Jesus" who always makes us feel okay about ourselves. If we believe this, we are living only one piece of the gospel.

When the pendulum swings the other way, the

picture is that of an angry, wrathful God. To the people who hold this view, God is perpetually mad at the world and can't wait to smite us when we get out of line. And so we respond in kind with a pious, compassionless moralism, enacting legislation to keep known sinners far away from us—lest we be struck by a stray thunderbolt.

We don't like tension though, let's face it. It's easier to pitch our tent in one camp or the other. We look for a God that fits our sensibilities. If we don't want to hear that we need to change our ways, we tend to camp with the "buddy Jesus" folks. On the other hand, if we consider ourselves to be pretty moral and we hate people who are not, we run with the "angry God" people. Yet both of these camps are built on a lie; their picture of God is based on a half-truth. To confine our view of Jesus to either extreme is to misunderstand the meaning of redemption.

THE GOOD, THE BAD, AND THE UGLY

Foundational to an accurate understanding of redemption is that the holy and righteous God who hates sin is also the merciful lover. Our attempts to marginalize him, to place him neatly into one of the two camps, are indicative of our foolish desire to control God. Control is always the nature of sin. I have to admit that I, too, want a God I can control rather than one who is in control. I may not say it out loud, but it's there. It's present in the choices I

make. My actions clearly show that I would rather
have a God who will give me the kind of life I think
I need. Jesus won't let me, though. He will never
bow to me, and I am really grateful for that. But it's
in my wiring somewhere. I function too often
believing that Jesus is there to do what I want him
to do. Thus the pendulum swings.

Jesus does not fight me for control. He is God; he
is in control. He simply waits for me to come to my
senses, lay down my own tainted picture of him, and
pick up the real picture that keeps him in the place of
tension. Loving and merciful, holy and righteous.
Fully God and fully God.

Yet we, as humans, have a capacity for denial that
is dangerous. Most of us are willing to embrace a half-
truth about God, even if the Bible explains clearly that
what we believe is a lie. The Bible lays out in plain
detail all that God is, even if we see it as the good, the
bad, and the ugly of his divine character. The Bible
does not candy-coat the facts or make God less than
he is. But we do, which is a clear indicator that we
don't want redemption; we want the power to make
God in the image we're *comfortable* with.

The irony is that in doing this we are trying to
redeem Jesus. But Jesus came to redeem *us*. In doing
so, he embodied the fullness of God in himself,
including all his holiness and hatred of sin alongside
the love and mercy of God toward a people ruined by
sin. Jesus held these two extreme truths in perfect
harmony. Jesus lived in that tension and was not

afraid of it, to the point of taking that tension to the cross.

We tend to think of the margins as a place for some people but not all people. The people who are broken and sinful and disenfranchised are marginalized, and people who are successful and happy are not. The lie in all of this is that we believe only *some* people need redemption. This leads to a second, more insidious lie: believing that we can one day better ourselves to the point where we are no longer in need of redeeming grace.

When we tear down the economic walls and strip away the nice homes, the expensive toys, and even the exclusive vacation hideaways in paradise, we *all* have sin and brokenness eating away at us on the inside. There are plenty of bad days going on in every soul, no matter who you are.

Success in this world does not mean acceptance before God. The Bible tells us that every one of us stands guilty of sin in relationship to God. To be confused on this point is to miss redemption. You will not stand among a company of your peers to be declared fit for heaven.

Your friends won't vote you into heaven, and they can't vote you out.

Only God can make that decision.

When I first became a Christ-follower I did not understand this. I believed that some people could be good enough that they don't need God. But the more I explored the Bible, the more I came to see that, in God's eyes, we *all* need redemption because we *all* have sin. God does not wink at our sin and look the other way; nor is he waiting to pounce on our every sin and dole out his prodigious wrath.

God hates our sin. But sin is in us. It is part of us and we can't shake it. It shows up in our actions, our thoughts, and our attitudes. At its core, sin is our desire to run our own lives any way we want. God hates that. He just does. He is not like you and me in that sin is not natural for him. It is the complete opposite of his holy character.

THE HIGH COST OF SIN

The word *holy* simply means "set apart." God is set apart from everything sinful. He is holy. The end result of our sin is that our relationship with him is broken off. We deserve to be punished by God. This sucks but it's true. And this means we have a problem we can't fix.

I remember sitting in front of my television set one Saturday watching the space shuttle explode during its descent into the atmosphere. Somewhere during the trip into space, something went wrong. The end result was the destruction of the shuttle and the death of the crew members. There was some awareness at mission control that a small piece of the spacecraft had broken off during takeoff. It didn't seem like a big deal at the time. But it was. It was a matter of life and death. And that's how sin is.

Today our culture is inoculated to sin. We are surrounded by it every day; it is in our society and in us. We see it and think it's no big deal. But it is a big deal. It is a matter of life and death.

Dismissing our sin as a small, insignificant part of life that is not functioning well will only result in our own destruction.

Amazingly, God is also compassionate and merciful and has a love for us that is beyond anything we could ever experience apart from him. And so God set out in Christ to purchase us back to himself. His hatred of our sin and his merciful love toward us were both manifested at the same time on the cross. Jesus died as our substitute, meaning that instead of punishing us for our sins, he punished Jesus instead. Jesus willingly went to the cross so that both his love for us could be manifested and the holiness of God could be satisfied.

In that single act of sacrifice, Isaiah 53:10 says, it was the Father's will to "crush him." He was pleased to punish his Son because his holiness demanded it. He was pleased to punish his Son because it meant that we, as his children, could be declared innocent before him. Christ's perfect life was given up to redeem us back to God. And with the power that only God has, Christ arose from the dead and overcame the greatest enemy of humanity: physical death.

The good, the bad, and the ugly of God—his mercy *and* his wrath—were displayed in perfect unity.

The tension this created is now parked in our camp. So what do we do with Jesus?

THIS IS NOT MY LIFE TO TAKE

Like an addict who's been freed from addiction but hasn't been told how to otherwise fill the void with love and meaning, I spent several years of my journey with Jesus thinking, *He did his part; now I need to figure out the rest.* I failed many times in my attempts to be perfect, trying to make myself acceptable to God. His grace was not something I felt comfortable receiving. In fact I fought it.

And so I carried the weight of my sin, stumbling again and again and sinking deeper into depression. I thought of killing myself.

I knew that God loved me and gave his Son for me, but I honestly thought it was a ridiculous transaction. How could Jesus give up his unblemished life for my sin-soaked existence that seemed to lack any meaning or hope? I would not allow it! I decided that, instead of accepting such extravagant grace, I would pay the penalty for my own sin. I would take my life.

But in that dark hour, God broke through to me. He reminded me of the words, "You are not your own; you were bought at a price" (1 Corinthians 6:19–20). And it struck me, *This is not my life to take; it's God's.* It is not simply in his possession, but it is *his* life, his Spirit, now living in me. He paid for me, in full, and he was giving me a life that was better than I could ever hope to get on my own. My job was not to be perfect, but to let him have the reins of my heart and life. My sins had been paid for, yes, but much more, I had become God's possession. Now it was time to reimagine life on God's terms, not mine.

I admit, I am a slow learner. It's like I own two pairs of glasses through which I see the world totally differently. My own lenses tend to focus on myself— making enough money to retire in paradise; getting everyone to think I'm a pretty important guy; and so on. The other lenses I have are the lenses of faith. They are the glasses given to me by Jesus. Through them I see a reality of life that is more real than sunny days in Mexico, more meaningful than living the good life. Every day Jesus invites me to see life through him, to reimagine what life really is. I find it all pretty simple when I choose to believe. Just as I find it really frustrating when I look only through my own lenses.

Grace. It keeps coming my way, even when I fail, and slowly I am learning to accept it. Gradually, my appetite for Christ's life grows and the bitter taste of sin fades. I can't say there are no bad days. But I do know this: The eternal God, who sent his Son to die in my place to free me from sin and to live his life, knows I like beaches. And he has something far better than an earthly paradise for me.

And for you.

COSMIC QUESTIONS

I am thirsty. My soul is thirsty. I can drink in all the world has to offer me, and I am still thirsty. It is this thirst that leads me to ask, What is the point of life? A longing that never gets filled? Jumping from one stream to another and another but never finding what I am looking for?

Each of us is on a quest to find meaning. It's part of our emotional DNA. Look around the margins and you see people scurrying about to find meaning like children on a scavenger hunt. We're running after things and sex and popularity and power. But nothing seems to last, as though every answer comes with an expiration date. Once you have found what you were looking for, the expiration date runs out and off you go again on the quest for meaning.

I have drunk from so many streams that left a bitter taste of sin in my mouth. *No life in this one. Maybe the next one will have it.* Have you been there?

The margins lack meaning. Jesus came to the margins to redeem us, but he then teaches us that the meaning of our life *is* Jesus. It means we must go to him to quench our thirsty hearts. That's a nice thought, but what does it mean?

In the book of Jeremiah, God says that his people have committed two sins. First, they have rejected Him, the fountain of living water. And second, they have dug for themselves broken cisterns that cannot hold water. God paints an amazing picture here of our quest for meaning. A cistern is a vessel for holding water. In that day, water was not as close as your kitchen sink. You had to walk to the nearest well and carry it back. If you had a cistern at home, you could fill it up and not have to go to the well every time you needed a cup of water. It would be right there.

God uses this illustration to show how we seek life in other things, all the while rejecting God, the very source of life. This is sin and it painfully shows the futility of our efforts. We spend an enormous amount of energy scurrying about finding water. When we finally do find it, we head for home to pour it into our cistern. We may have spent hours upon hours trying to get it, and we cannot wait to be home, secure with our water, not having to search and work for it anymore. Our thirst can be immediately satisfied anytime. But when we pour the water out into the cistern, the cistern is full of cracks. It's broken. The water slowly seeps out through the cracks and back into the ground. We can only stand there watching the water leak out, while the sweat from our labor is still on our foreheads.

This is what it looks like to spend our days searching for meaning outside of God. And while we are so busy seeking, carrying, and laboring over this water that is so elusive and deceptive in its allure, God calls to us, "I am right over here—a fountain of pure living water. No working. Your search is over. There is a constant flow of life here. You will find the satisfaction you seek. Come and drink!"

And yet we continue to look elsewhere.

CREATING OUR OWN REALITY

Our culture tells us to create our own meaning. "Find a hobby or a career that makes you happy. And if your marriage isn't making you happy, don't waste your life, man. Leave her for someone else!" I talked to a guy who was leaving his wife and kids; he told me it was time for him to focus on his own happiness.

Our culture teaches that *you* are the most important person in *your* universe, so find *your own* meaning. And try not to hurt others on the way. But the problem with this approach is twofold: We always hurt others with our selfish pursuits, and still we never find fulfillment.

Create my own meaning? I get question marks churning in the pit of my stomach just thinking about it. What is the meaning of life? How do I know? I have enough trouble paying my bills and getting to work on time. And the world is ready with no-hassle, mix-and-match, microwaveable solutions available on easy credit terms. The seduction is all around us: "Come and drink. We know just what you're thirsty for. Unsure of what you want your life to mean? Try a little of this, a little of that. If you don't see anything you like, there's more in the back. Come and drink."

Our culture is full of cheap prostitutes that promise to relieve our emptiness. We don't have to go far to be invited to a false fountain.

TECHNO TOYS

Technology is one of the allurements that promises to complete us. My TV is too small. If only I had a big-screen with surround sound, *that* would fulfill me. I could play my Xbox on it, and the characters on the games would be three feet tall! Then I would look forward to coming home. Then I could relax.

Technology holds out promises that it can't meet. Don't get me wrong; I love my toys. I love my Palm and my thin laptop. My MP3 player is an amazing tool—five thousand songs on a sleek-looking unit that's no bigger than a deck of cards. Technology is incredible, at least until my computer crashes or I drop my MP3 player. Then technology sucks. But the first day you purchase a new toy, you don't care what else is going on; then after a week the high wears off and you're looking through the sale ads again.

Everyone assumed that technological innovation would make life better, simpler, and in many ways it has. I like having electricity; no complaints there. I am grateful that I can take my kids to the hospital if they're sick or injured and that the doctors have lots of little machines that can help them get better.

But technology has its limits. It cannot answer that daunting question, What is the point of my life? <u>Technology can create enough noise so we don't hear the question being screamed at us, but it can't remove the desperate longing.</u> Once you unplug, then where are you? Watching the water flow through the cracks.

HERE WE ARE, NOW ENTERTAIN US

Entertainment is pretty good at numbing the question. I love to laugh, and I love to play. I love movies, and I like just vegging out. I love going to a ball game or concert. Billions of dollars are spent every year to get you to try the latest, greatest theme-park ride or TV sitcom, with promises that these things will make you happy. And they do, for a time. But like a small dose of heroin, we need more pretty quick or we get bored. And it takes a bigger dose each time to really make an impact on us.

Boredom comes across as the great sin of our day. Heaven forbid that we should ever get bored. Why do we get bored? I think it happens when we've watched the water run out of our entertainment cistern. Then we're left just standing there, looking around for the next stream of water with a flashy sign and the promise to make us happy. We're becoming passive spectators of life who need someone else to tell us who we are and what we like. We get lazy and let other people tell us what the meaning of life is. And we don't question whether they're right, because just for a moment they made us laugh.

Then we awake a few hours later with empty cisterns.

PLEASURE AND APPETITES

I remembering watching MTV's *Cribs,* a show where they take the viewer through the houses of celebrities. These houses are incredible! More bedrooms than you will ever use. Pools with waterfalls, garages full of sweet cars. These people have everything. And if they don't have it, they can buy it. As I sat in my small house, looking out the window at my two cars with lots of miles on them, I found myself *wanting.* I wanted their homes and cars and money. I thought that those things would give me life.

Beneath that kind of desire is a deceptive stream calling out, "I can make you happy. This will complete you." Too many times I've believed that. When I look at the lifestyles of the rich and famous, I see Pleasure. These people fly on a whim to beautiful, exotic places and hang with beautiful people. Man, I wish I were beautiful.

The thing about Pleasure is that she taps into our flesh in a way few things can. It feels good. Really good. But Pleasure goes away. She touches us for a moment, and in that moment the rest of the world fades away and we think life is good. But then the moment's over and the party ends. The cash runs out, Pleasure loses her power, and I am left to be alone with me. And the emptiness.

Pleasure deceives us into believing that she holds the keys to life. Most of us are Pleasure seekers. When we hang our hope on Pleasure to give our lives meaning, we spend the bulk of our time looking down at an empty cistern. We are quick to pick up the pots of our hearts and scurry off to find another well full of pleasure. Pretty soon, though, your legs get heavy and you get tired of looking.

That's why if I turn the channel to VH1, I can watch *Where Are They Now?* This show is about performers who had it all and then lost it. The program describes in detail the emptiness that follows a few moments of pleasure. These one-time celebrities awoke one day to find their fifteen minutes of fame were up. People quit buying their music or going to see their movies, and they soon realized that the water had run out the bottom—and they were left still wondering what the meaning of life is.

INFORMATION AGE

Knowledge promises to give us life. If we have the right degree, we can get the best jobs. If we just had the right information, we could solve the world's problems, or at least our own. If I knew how to have meaning in my life then I would have it, right? We live in a time when we have more knowledge than we know what to do with. Most of us are educated beyond our potential. Yet there is still a numbing emptiness.

The Internet promised everyone would have access to knowledge. There should no longer be a knowledge gap between those who can afford information and those who can't. Now our personal computers connect us to all the facts and information we can handle. That should have solved our problems, right? Instead, there is a growing skepticism about what is true. Who says it's true? You can hardly prove your point by saying, "I read it on the Internet." That's not saying much. Knowledge doesn't mean much if what we know is not true.

The allure of knowledge is also deceptive because

so many believe that when they get the knowledge then they will be able to readily apply it. Then we find out that our family doctor smokes a pack a day. A local pastor has an affair. *Why would they do that?* Don't these people know that these are the wrong things to do? Yes, they know. They just don't believe it. Information does not guarantee transformation. Knowing what the meaning of life is and living a life of meaning are not the same thing.

We see this especially in the church. We've believed for so long that knowing about God is the same as knowing God. So we rush off to Bible studies and Bible college and seminary. We think that we are accumulating knowledge and that will fix us. If we master this book of the Bible or that theology, then we will really know God and our lives will change. But our information piles up and transformation is slow to happen. Why? Because knowledge is a deceptive stream, even though the stream is promising us God. We watch the water seep through the cracks and our stack of theology books fall over.

We have made knowledge our God and tried to master God as a subject instead of Savior. An empty cistern. God never intended to lie down on our dissection tables and let us cut him open to study his parts. The lie is that we believe God is simply the sum of his parts. So we think we have mastered God, only to find that he got off the table and left the building. To know something, in God's mind, is to have a relationship with it, not to kill it and study its parts.

God says to Jeremiah, "My people have committed two sins: They have forsaken me, the spring of living water, and have dug their own cisterns, broken cisterns that cannot hold water." Technology, entertainment, pleasure, knowledge—all these are mirages on the quest to fill an empty heart. They promise to give life that they know nothing of. They are nothing more than illusions—mere deceptions that will ultimately steal, kill, and destroy.

If we spend our lives banking on one or more of these things to give our life meaning, we end up losing the life we sought to gain. The deception is that instead of gaining something, we are robbed of something. Instead of living, we are dying. Instead of building, we are being destroyed. And we find ourselves stuck in the margins. Disappointment invades the margins daily as we trust in things that promise real meaning—but in the morning put their pants on and are gone. And we're left waiting in the margins. Thirsty again.

DRINKING OF THE WATER OF LIFE

God hates that. He did not create us to fall victim to deception and destruction. Jesus invites us out of the margins to discover the meaning of life in relationship with him. "If anyone is thirsty, let him come to me and drink," he says to us. "Whoever believes in me, as the Scripture has said, streams of living water will flow from within him" (John 7:37–38). The fountain of living water.

Jesus makes this claim at the Feast of Tabernacles, when all of Israel has come to Jerusalem to celebrate God's provision for them as a people. God had redeemed them out of slavery in Egypt and provided for them on their journey to the Promised Land. Every morning of the weeklong feast, there is a ceremony in which the religious leaders march in procession carrying a gold pitcher full of water they have drawn from a pool called Siloam. They then pour out the water at the temple to commemorate how God provided water for them in the wilderness by making water flow out of rock. God has instituted this feast so that every year his people will come together to remember that he is their source of life. And it is amid this scene that Jesus stands up and in a loud voice says, "If anyone is thirsty, let him come to me and drink! Whoever believes in me, as the Scripture has said, streams of living water will flow from within him."

This is a bold claim. But in this setting, it is one the people can understand. As much as this is a feast for remembering, it is also a time for envisioning. For looking forward to the time when God will send the Messiah. The Scriptures speak of a time when God will be with his people and will fill them with himself.

Thus Jesus unveils himself to them. He asks, "Is anyone thirsty?" The people in the audience that day are no different from us. They, too, look for life in many other streams. Yet they are still thirsty. They have dug their own cisterns and found that they leak. Their streams are different from ours, but the end result is the same. All their efforts yield only false life that seeps through the cracks of their hearts and leaves them thirsty.

"Come to me and drink."

How do we do that? Jesus says that we need to believe in him. But what does that mean exactly? We have turned belief into little more than a cognitive assent to something we think is probably true. That is not a biblical understanding of belief. The Bible speaks of belief as an *active response* to something we know is true. When Jesus says to believe in him, to believe that he is the source of life, he is not merely asking us to nod our heads in agreement with him. He is telling us to bank our life on him in relationship. That he *is* life.

Elsewhere Jesus says that he is "the resurrection and the life." He makes this statement as a prelude to performing one of the greatest miracles ever: He brings his dead friend Lazarus back to life. Lazarus has been dead for four days. Friends and family members are standing around the tomb, weeping and mourning, when Jesus tells the people to roll back the stone. The mourners are shocked at this. After all, decomposition would have begun to set in by now. But they do it anyway and Jesus yells, "Lazarus, come forth!" Moments later, Lazarus comes walking out with his grave clothes hanging off him. And jaws drop all around.

The miracle is not the point of the story, though. The miracle points to the claim that Jesus makes about himself: "He who believes in me will live, even though he dies; and whoever lives and believes in me will never die" (John 11:25–26).

Jesus essentially says, "I am the meaning of life and the answer to death." Only the one who conquered death has the authority to tell us what life is supposed to be all about.

To all of us thirsty margin dwellers, Jesus shows up with incredible news: *The life that you seek, a life of meaning and love, is found in relationship with me. Come to me and drink of my love.* Jesus gives us meaning every day as we live life through him and for him and, most importantly, with him. Jesus redeems us *to* something—a new life. He calls us to remember and envision and reimagine life through the lens of his words.

Our quest to find meaning in other places only leaves us thirsty and staring at an empty cistern. All the while, Jesus offers himself as a fountain of living water so that we might drink deeply from the source of all life. He created your heart and knows what it longs for. What you crave can only be found in him.

All other streams will leave you with a dry mouth and a thirsty soul.

Quit seeking and drink. Enter into his love and trust moment by moment that he is all you need. Choose to live under his care and in the truth. That is what active belief looks like, drinking in the grace and mercy, acceptance and forgiveness that he gives. Live wisely, knowing that the sparkle of the world's toys is deceptive and that your heart's desire cannot be fulfilled by them. You were made to find meaning in Jesus. He is life. His love will not seep out of your heart, but keeps flowing so you will never be thirsty again.

Do you believe?

UNTAMED LOVE

I remember my words bouncing off her forehead as I said them: "God loves you!" She had been raised in the church and was in her early twenties, and she had read the Bible for as long as she could remember. Still, my words could not penetrate the walls she had erected to protect her heart from being hurt again.

She told me of the sexual abuse she had endured as a young girl and that she now struggles with not giving her body to others. What was taking place inside her was a much greater struggle. It was a battle for her soul. Jesus was inviting her to trust him, to move out of this marginal place and into his love, but she was struggling to buy it. Why? She didn't believe she was loveable. And so she could not receive the love of Jesus. People in the margins often struggle to receive his love because they do not believe that they can be loved.

In the margins we exchange the true love of Jesus and a life of pure acceptance for cheap substitutes. We all need to be loved. It's like water—we can't live without it.

When we have given up on the idea of being loved and accepted for who we are, we go after a generic brand of love—something to medicate the pain inside our hearts. We may try one-night stands, look for it in pornography, or pursue the fleeting freedom of alcohol or drugs. We may even use busyness to fill the void. Staying busy at church so we don't have to cope with loneliness is another way people in the margins polish up their pain so others will believe they have it all together.

Whatever the avenue, the margins are full of people scrambling to get love, all the while knowing it is not a love that will satisfy. The tragedy in the margins is that we numbly accept this as our reality. Because underneath the layers of these actions lurks the real enemy: the belief that we can't be loved.

COMFORTABLY NUMB

Jesus has been chasing after marginalized people like you and me for hundreds of years. His invitation is simple: "Trust me when I tell you I love you, and trust me to help you reimagine life in my love."

But Jesus is an untamed lover. Perhaps that's why I am tempted to avoid his kind of love. I want a love I can tame. I don't want it to take me where I don't want to go. But Jesus will have no part in that cheap exchange.

He wants all of me—sin, shame, and pain.

He won't let me live in my brokenness and be happy. He is unwilling that I should buy into the lies of the world and its cheap substitutes. Instead, his untamed love takes me to the end of myself where I can fully know and experience his love.

The destructive power of the margins lies in their ability to convince us to be comfortable in our numbness. The margins weaken our desire for a better life. If we can feed our love-hungry souls with those counterfeit vices, we're likely to stay put. C. S. Lewis observed that God finds our desires too weak, not too strong. We fool about with sex and drink while infinite love awaits us. We're like children in the ghetto making mud pies because we cannot fathom what a holiday at sea would mean.

What are we avoiding?

Most of us grew up too fast and learned through painful circumstances that we cannot bank on being loved for who we are. Part of the journey out of the margins and into love takes us through a forest where Jesus asks us to rethink what we believe about our lovability. Sometimes that means addressing painful things that taught us we can't be loved. We need to face our painful pasts head-on so that we come out the other end believing that God's love for us is truer than the lies that pain taught us.

Personally, I don't like pain. Physical pain, emotional pain, any kind of pain. I'm a wuss that way. I guess most of us are. When you think about pain in life, particularly life in the margins, there is way too much of it. You see it in poverty among little children. You see it in the suffering of people who are dying. You see it when one person takes out his sin on another. You see it in people stuck in sin. You see it deep within the hearts of those who live in the margins.

That soft heart you were born with, while sinful, was still tender toward life. Children hope and feel; they have joy, they play. But something about growing up and the harsh reality of life teaches us that we need to protect ourselves. When pain came calling—the first kid who made fun of you, an alcoholic parent, a divorce—we tried to protect ourselves. It's a natural reaction.

But after years of protecting ourselves we develop a hard shell around our heart so no one can get in, so no one can hurt us or take advantage of us again. That is a margin. When you can't reach out to be loved by God and other people because you're holding your arms up defensively like a prizefighter, you're living in a margin.

To live that way is not to really live, though. We go through the motions of life, but we don't really go through the *e*motions of life. The pain we've experienced is numbed by the hard shell covering our heart. Any joy that comes our way is viewed with skepticism born of a suspicion that any good thing, any relationship that invites me to love and be loved, probably has a false motive. We may even distort God's love by telling ourselves, *God is only loving me because he wants something from me.*

So we protect ourselves and we think this diminished life is somehow "normal."

THE LIE OF SELF-PROTECTION

The problem with protecting your heart from pain is that a barricaded heart won't let any good things in, either, things like love and joy. Some of us use humor as a defense mechanism: We make fun of things that are full of life, and we question people's motives and their goodness. Eventually a layer of cynicism covers our heart like a callus. It's a natural response to life gone bad in places, and it's a one-way ticket to life in the margins.

Self-protection is false protection. Believing that you can guard your heart is believing a lie. Because that hard shell will not protect your heart; it will actually kill your heart. It's like taking a rosebush indoors, away from the weather, in the hopes that if you remove it from the harsh realities of the rain and the scorching sun and stick it in a dark and secure space within your house, then the plant will be protected and will grow. True, on the one hand the roses will not be blown away by the wind, or frostbitten on cold nights, or shrivel in the heat of the sun. But in that dark and secure place the rosebush cannot grow, because the place of darkness and isolation doesn't have sunlight and the other life-giving properties required for growing healthy roses. The things the rosebush needs can only be found out there in the world where there also exists the possibility of exposure to harsh elements.

Likewise, the self-protective measures we think are saving us are actually killing us. We place our hearts in a dark closet, away from the harsh realties of the world, but in that place the heart begins to wither. I don't want to make light of the pain that puts us there, though. When someone hurts us or rejection leaves us broken, it only makes sense that we never want to let *that* happen again. And so we hide our hearts away, only to find ourselves huddled in the margins with our arms folded across our chest. There the heart can no longer take in the things we so desperately need—love, joy, peace, kindness, trust. That's why I define it as life in the margins, because it so limits our experience of life.

DIANE'S STORY

My friend Diane is one of the brave souls who has accepted Christ's invitation to leave the margins and reimagine life through his love. Jesus found her in the margins and, layer by layer, removed the walls of self-protection she had put up around her heart.

Diane grew up in a home most of us could not imagine. Diane's father was physically and emotionally abusive. His anger would flare up constantly, and he would beat his daughter and tell her horrible things about herself. The only thing that held Diane's life together was the loving presence of her mom. She was a strong, protective, nurturing influence—but when Diane was five years old, her mom died. You can imagine what it might be like for a little girl to lose her mother and sole protector. Soon after, Diane's grandmother also became ill and died, leaving her in the care of a father who beat her and a grandfather who began sexually abusing her.

The brutal reality of other people's sin took its toll on the tender heart of this child. Her life was torture, and Diane developed a protective layer over her heart to hold back the pain. Just when it seemed like her world couldn't get any worse, it did. Her father remarried, bringing into the home an emotionally abusive woman who, just like Diane's father, had a volatile temper and cruel nature.

Life taught Diane not to trust anyone or anything because bad things were going to happen and the good people whom she loved would be taken away from her. She learned not to like herself because the very people God ordained to be in authority over her told her she was bad and deserved punishment; she deserved to be beaten and used as a tool for their self-gratification. Implicit in all of this was the ultimate lesson that the world is a very scary and dangerous place and so Diane must protect herself.

Eventually, Diane grew up and got married to an amazing man, had two beautiful daughters, and apparently coped with her childhood very well, because if you had met Diane, you would have known her to be the most giving, loving, bubbly person. She would throw parties where she would love and give herself fully to her guests. But the underlying reality was that she wasn't *receiving* love. She could not receive God's grace and acceptance and all the good things he wanted to give her. Diane simply could not trust because she didn't want to be hurt again.

But as Jesus came more and more deeply into Diane's life, he began to pull back the layers covering her heart, exposing a very, very tender wound. A wound that she had not wanted to look at or deal with. A wound that she had just wanted to make go away. Sometimes pulling back those layers feels like you're ripping your flesh off, but Jesus in his goodness and grace was relentless, knowing that while Diane may have thought she was protecting herself, all the while inside her heart was dying.

A lot of us are like Diane, not wanting to have that layer peeled back because we believe that underneath there lies an immense amount of pain—pain that we have caused ourselves, pain that's been caused by others, or pain that life has dealt us through the brutal realities of death or suffering. But Jesus doesn't see the world as you and I see it; he understands that although our pain is very real, it is not more real than his love.

Nor is pain more powerful than his love.

In his grace Jesus pursues us to the margins to pull back the layers of self-protection, because he knows that if we live our entire life with our hearts hidden away in the darkness we'll simply shrivel up and die inside. The numbness we've fashioned for ourselves cannot give birth to life. That numbness, that callousness, keeps us from receiving the love he has for us; and if we can't receive his love, then we can't know his healing. In short, unless he strips away the barrier around our hearts, we cannot begin our journey out of the margins to reimagine life in his love.

DIANE'S TRANSFORMATION

When Jesus began to pull down the walls around Diane's heart, certain things were very difficult for her to face, not to ignore the pain but to agree that these terrible things happened to her.

By God's grace, Diane was able to forgive—forgive her dad, forgive her grandfather, and forgive her stepmother for the abuse that had taken place. She was able to be named by God as his child, as one he had redeemed. And perhaps more important, she began to receive. She was able to hear Jesus say to her, "Diane, I love you. You are my child."

Through this process, Diane definitely struggled. It was not an easy road. There were times of stumbling, faltering. But time and again Jesus reached out his hand to pull Diane up. No only did she discover and come to believe that Jesus loved her, but she became a conduit of his love to others. Diane was used by God to bring others out of the margins and into his love.

Diane spent her mornings with her journal and her Bible, praying and listening to the Word of God. She communed daily with the Spirit of God, journaling the truth that God was revealing to her. God loved her. God cherished her. She was God's redeemed and beautiful daughter.

The transformation that took place in Diane's life was one of the most miraculous I have ever seen. Diane spent the last fifteen years of her life giving herself away to other people, taking the love she received from Jesus and giving it away to other people who were hurting, whose hearts still bore deep wounds. God used her to be his healing hands in the lives of so many to encourage them to trust in Jesus' love.

I met with Diane almost every week and she became one of the great mentors I've known, teaching me how to walk into the arms of Christ. She would say to me over and over, as God was peeling away the layer on my own heart, "Will you dare to trust? Will you dare to believe?" She held my hand as I traveled the journey out of unbelief and into the love of Jesus.

Diane showed me what courage looked like as she walked through those difficult places in her life and let Jesus become her forgiver and healer in those places. She dared to trust, dared to believe, dared to be what God intended her to be. That is real transformation, whereby God changes us from hurting, self-protecting people into his lovers, and Diane was perhaps the most powerful lover of Jesus that I've ever witnessed. Simply because she chose to take him at his word: His love for her was greater than the pain she had experienced. Jesus had pulled Diane out of the margins and into his love.

DIANE'S EXAMPLE

Diane and her husband, Paul, became two of our closest friends, and they helped us start a church, a community of faith called Imago Dei Community. Then two years into our adventure, at the age of fifty-two, Diane was diagnosed with Lou Gehrig's disease.

During the last year of her life, Diane began to slowly wither away physically, but she didn't retreat into that place of self-protection. She no longer needed to reimagine life through Jesus; she had become fully adept at living in the reality of it day by day. She listened to the voice of God, read his Word, and wrote down over and over what it meant to be loved by Jesus. Though Death stood nearby, biding his time, Diane had banked her trust and hope in this greatest love of all. The One who had come to her in the margins and pulled her out of that place, he had transformed her from someone who lived in fear and self-protection into a lover of God and a lover of people.

I remember sitting with Diane and having her pray for me. Hearing her talk to Jesus reminded me of someone speaking to a friend. She was full of trust and belief that God would meet me in the margins of my own life and invite me to believe his love for me. She had become other-centered, fully attentive to the whispers of the soul in communion with God.

In her hour of greatest need, that last year of her life, Diane was an inspiration to our church. She was like a mother to so many in our body. She had taught us what it meant to be loved by God and, in that nurturing way that God had gifted her with, she was the catalyst that God used to pull back the layers from so many hearts. She invited us to reimagine life through Jesus by modeling what that life could be. She told us that his love was for us and that he had given us a new life filled with his love.

On October 3, 2003, Diane went home to be with Jesus. I remember those final days, sitting by her bedside and telling her that I was going to dedicate this book to her memory. And she smiled this smile that only Diane could give and said, "Wow, I've never had a book dedicated to me before!"

But I know Diane's name is written in God's book, the most important book of all, and I believe she stands today in that beautiful place, face-to-face with the One who loves her like no other could. The One who taught her that although life is scary, although bad things are going to happen, although pain is going to show up, the deeper things of God are also in that place and all she had to do was open her hands to receive the love of Jesus.

As you think about yourself walking out of the margins and into this place of relationship with Jesus, he asks you to believe that he loves you. Your life and mine may be nowhere near as difficult as Diane's was, but we all know something of what it means to be marginalized. We all have a deep, aching thirst that can only be satisfied by pursuing and being pursued by the living Christ.

In Galatians 5 the apostle Paul tells us what it means to be filled with the Spirit, to truly experience life in the light of God's love. Paul specifically mentions being given love, joy, peace, patience, kindness, faithfulness, gentleness, and self-control—qualities we could never grasp or know when staring at life through the lens of self-protection. And if we stand before others with our hands wrapped tightly around our hearts, protecting ourselves, then we'll never experience these wondrous emotions that we were created to enjoy. We'll never understand what it means to let the tender place in our soul be exposed, to offer ourselves to others, to love them, to bring them joy, to be gentle and kind toward them, to be patient with them.

Only Jesus can transform us from self-protecting people into tender lovers of God and lovers of others. The power of Christ is that in his mission to the margins he came to redeem and forgive and ultimately to transform. It's only when we're willing to invite Jesus into those places in our hearts and say, "Go ahead and expose it; I'm no longer going to protect myself from you" that his deep work in our lives can begin. Frankly, nothing on our spiritual journey is going to make a lot of sense if we cannot first receive the love that God has for us and to dare to believe that his word stands above all our circumstances, above all abuse, above all of our pain and trust that he has the final word in our lives.

When I was twenty-three years old, I believed that God could not love me. It was a lie that was imbedded in my soul. It's not that I didn't know the Bible taught that God loved me; I just didn't believe it. Instead, I would try to fill the void with eating or working hard so that people would think I was really great. The whole time I was betraying the deepest love I had ever experienced, the love of Jesus Christ. I was running about after mud pies because I couldn't fathom Jesus' love for me. When it finally hit me that Jesus really loved me, that the good news of the gospel was true for me, too, the weight of "performing" for love just blew away. Suddenly sin and its seductive voice seemed so much weaker. The chains of the margins were slowly unleashing me as I came to realize that God was inviting me—*me!*—to be transformed into his child.

I wish I could say that I never went back to feeling unlovable. I daily fight the struggle of faith. I have to stand against the lies that my past and my sin tell me to believe. But the more I live in this place of faith, the more the words of Christ make sense to me: "The truth will set you free" (John 8:32).

I no longer need to appease my hunger for love with cheap substitutes, because Jesus meets me and asks me to reimagine life in his love.

Will you let Jesus peel back the layers and expose your tender heart? Are you ready to receive his love for you? Are you ready to reimagine life by believing that you, too, are loved by God?

FATHER OF MINE

Something about the word *father* brings to mind a picture—a picture that differs for each of us, according to our experience. Some people see a grinning face cheering on the sidelines during a youth soccer game. Some people see a birthday card showing up a month late with a five-dollar bill inside. Some people see a guy who slept with their mom, and moved on. For too many of us our experience of *father* is limited to images of Cliff Huxtable and Tony Soprano.

In the margins you find a lot of people who have little or no relationship with their dads. In the margins, *father* is often a four-letter word. I could never understand why God chose to call himself Father. He knew that many people would misunderstand what he meant by it, so why did he choose it?

The reality is that in the early dawn of this new millennium, ours is a fatherless generation. The evidence is found in the scarred hearts of people in the margins. These are the scars of abandonment left by the wounds of divorce, abuse, and dads who disengaged emotionally from their families.

Fathers have tremendous power to shape our lives, a power inherent in the family structure as ordained by God. God designed the father to be the head of the home, and so each of us is wired to long for the love of our fathers. When fathers abuse their God-given place in our lives, they leave a legacy of confusion and heartache for their children.

Countless young men and women are growing up right now without a real understanding of what the word *father* means. So many of us take *father* to mean the Homer Simpsons we see in the media—goofy and aloof guys who aren't really tuned in to their kids' lives and are not worthy of much respect.

Jesus tells us *father* means something else.

He invites us to reimagine life in relationship with the *perfect* Father. Jesus redeems us from our sin and the brokenness of our father-wounds, and he returns us to the Father and his love for us.

In order to reimagine life in the Father's love, we need to understand who this Father is and what he is like. If we don't, we will simply take our broken understanding of what a father is and attach it to God, and that will only leave us confused and angry with God. But Jesus wants to paint us a new picture of *father* so that we will know and believe that *his* Father is *our* Father. Then we can begin to live life in his perfect love.

So what *is* the Father like?

In Matthew 6, Jesus introduces us to his Father, describes what he is like, and lets us know how he feels about us. For one thing, Jesus tells us, the Father knows what we need even before we ask him. For many of us, prayer can be an awkward experience. Somebody once said it's hard to have a conversation with someone who already knows what you're going to say.

When I first began my spiritual journey with Christ, I thought about prayer all wrong. I believed that if I prayed long enough God would listen to me. If he looked down and saw my devotion then maybe he would pay attention to my needs. I had this mental picture of God as distant and aloof and avoiding me, waiting to see if I proved worthy of his attention. My early efforts at prayer were tainted by this false picture of the Father. But Jesus paints a new picture for us: The Father is *very* attentive to our needs—so attentive that he knows what they are before we ask.

Too often, we chalk that truth up to the fact that God knows everything, and we dismiss the reality of his desire for relationship. We tend to think of God as the ultimate computer containing all the data of life and creation in his hard drive. We depersonalize God and keep him at a distance, and so we remain unmoved by the truth of what Jesus is teaching.

Jesus is inviting us into a relationship. He says the

Father knows what you need before you ask not only because he's omnipotent, but because the Father is paying attention to the details of your life out of his great concern and deep love for you.

People in the margins struggle with this. Somewhere along the way they learned that they're not really valuable enough to pay attention to. Perhaps they were ignored by their fathers or unwanted by those who were placed in a position to care for them. Jesus wants you to know that you *are* valuable—that although your sin and brokenness have kept you away from God, Jesus has already paid the ultimate price to cover them. Now the Father wants you to see that he is in love with you and is paying close attention to the intimate needs and longings of your heart.

CHILD OF THE ETERNAL KING

In this same chapter of Matthew, Jesus teaches us how to pray to our attentive Father. The first line of his prayer reminds us that our Father reigns in heaven as ruler of an eternal kingdom. This is perhaps the toughest place for us to reimagine our lives. When we speak about kingdoms, we naturally go to the place of mythology. Stories flood the mind of princes and princesses and evil villains, and we are prone to set it all aside as fiction. But the Father's eternal kingdom is very real. More real then American democracy, more real than reigns of ter-

ror, and more real than your eight-to-five job. The
pinnacle of reality is God himself, and his reign in
the eternal kingdom is the greatest truth of all.

The implications for us are extreme when we
begin to reimagine life in the love of a Father who is
the eternal King: We belong to the only eternal King
and his kingdom lasts forever. That's our Father!

Yet tragically, many of us who claim to believe are
still stuck in the margins, wandering around with our
heads to the ground and acting like orphans with no
place to belong and no one to love. We are so named
by the sin and woundedness in our lives that we fail to
realize whose children we are.

One of my mentors, David Needham, tells the
story of a young prince. When he is still a small boy
his father's kingdom is invaded by hostile forces, and
so the guards of the palace take the prince away and
hide him in the slums of a neighboring kingdom.
There he grows up in the muck and mire of the
ghetto. Surrounded by violence and drugs and prosti-
tution, the young prince comes to believe that he is
merely an orphaned child with dirty clothes, living in
the streets.

When he turns thirteen, the palace guards come
to get him. They tell him the story of how they took
him away to protect him, but the war is now over and
the time has come to claim his rightful place on the
throne. That first night in the palace he looks at his
old clothes, torn and tattered, stained with the filth of
the streets. Then he looks at the royal robe that he is

meant to wear. Everything within him is telling him that he is not the child of a king. Not even close. He is an orphan from the ghetto. He knows the life he has lived and the things he grew up around. He is named by those things. But there is a deeper reality behind the appearances: He is a child of the king and royal blood flows through his veins. The young boy needs to reimagine life as a child of the king—a reality more true than his experience.

This is what Jesus is calling us to. Whatever your experience of life has been, the royal blood of Jesus was shed and is sufficient to bring you into relationship with your Father, who reigns in an eternal kingdom.

You are a child of the King.

You belong to him. It is time to throw away the old clothes of your brokenness and sin and begin to live under your Father's protection and provision.

Our Father, the Gracious Forgiver

I had a friend named Tim who sinned against his dad when we were growing up. He cut school repeatedly. His grades were pretty bad. He was partying too much and not going to class. Finally, his dad wrote him off. He disowned him. When my friend came home one day, he found the locks changed and his stuff on the front lawn. He was a junior in high school at the time, but was forced to drop out of school and get an apartment. I tried to talk to Tim about it, but he couldn't go there. It was a place of great pain for him. He knew he'd blown it when he lied to his father, but he never thought it would end in his being disowned.

What Tim learned was, *If you fail, you are a failure; and you need to perform to be my son.* In Matthew 9:14, Jesus tells us that our Father is gracious to forgive, but in the margins many of us have trouble receiving grace simply because it's alien to our experience. Even in the closest relationships, such as a father and son's, grace is too often a foreign substance. And when we come to believe we are not lovable, not forgivable, we are named with rejection.

Then Jesus invades the margins and finds us in this rejected and sinful state, and he reaches out and lifts up our chin and says, "I died for *you,* and my Father is ready to forgive and accept you!"

But God also requires us to *extend* forgiveness. Jesus says, "If you forgive men when they sin against you, your heavenly Father will also forgive you" (Matthew 6:14). One of the chains that keeps us anchored to the margins is the chain of unforgiveness. Like giant links wrapped around our chest and secured to the ground at the farthest side of the margins, unforgiveness assures us that we will not move to where we can reimagine life in the love of the Father.

Many of us desperately need to forgive our earthly dads. We were hurt; there is no question that injury has taken place. But God's answer is always to forgive. Not to take revenge, not to hold a grudge, not to seek payback or restitution. Most of the time, we did not deserve the pain that was inflicted on us, but that does not give us permission to withhold forgiveness from the party responsible. If you receive God's forgiveness, your heavenly Father commands you to forgive as well. The wounds in Jesus' hands and side are there for your father's sin, too.

But in order to forgive, you first must recognize and name the offense. *This happened to me!* Whatever it is. You need to articulate the effect that the pain had on your life. Then you need to set that person free to God: "Because my heavenly Father has forgiven my sin, Dad, I forgive you for what you did to me."

Allow the Father's love to break the chains of unforgiveness that leave you bound to the margins. Sweet freedom is waiting for you. Freedom to live in the gracious forgiveness of the Father.

AN INVOLVED FATHER

I remember hearing the panicked cry coming from outside.

"Dad! Da-a-ad!"

As a father you learn to recognize the unique sound of your child's cry. I quickly ran out to see what Zach needed. My six-year-old, Zach, was just learning to climb trees and was determined to make a go of it, despite a succession of skinned knees. Zach is a fighter, a competitive spirit. He refuses to give up and will persist till he wins.

That day, I found Zach perched high up in a tree in our yard. He had kept climbing to see how high he could go, never thinking about how he might get down. I could see in his tear-filled eyes the fear of falling. He had climbed up beyond his ability to get down.

"Don't worry, bud," I said, trying to reassure him. "I'm here. I won't let you fall." I climbed up and took Zach in my arms. I could feel him trembling as I told him to let go of the branch. His little heart was still pounding against my chest as I lowered him to the ground.

That day, Zach needed me and I was there. There will be times when I won't be able to be there for him like that. But at that moment I was involved and there to meet his immediate need.

Many of us grew up stuck high in our own trees, clinging to the tenuous branches of circumstance, painfully aware that we didn't have what it takes to get down on our own. Yet there was no one to cry out to because, for whatever reason, the people we depended on were not involved in our lives.

In the first chapter we saw a couple of snapshots from the margins that illustrate the problem of the uninvolved father. The first was from David. He never knew his dad, and so David had to figure out for himself what being a man is all about. The other was from Peter, the fifty-five-year-old businessman who made piles of cash but gave up his family in the process. These are just two snapshots of the uninvolved dad—

pictures that can stamp your heart as a child and leave you in the margins.

Growing up, we all have needs. And a lot of them can only be met by a father. When Dad decides to bail or is uninvolved, we become marked by a sense of abandonment that cements our feet in the margins. And when the details of life get messy, we long for a father who isn't there to come to our aid.

Then Jesus paints us a picture of a heavenly Father who is *deeply* involved in our daily affairs. In Matthew 6:25–26 he tells us not to worry about those things that we spend so much of our daily energy striving after— food, clothes, money, housing, to name just a few. Jesus tells us to take a lesson from nature. The birds of the air don't have houses, but God takes care of them.

Are we not much more valuable to our Father than the birds?

He says we are.

I am amazed each spring as I watch the robins invade our yard. Picking up fallen branches and tufts of grass, they build incredible nests where they lay their eggs and bring their young into the world. Who taught them that? I couldn't make a nest half as good, even though I have fingers and opposable thumbs. God cares for the robins, but he cares for you more.

The Father who provides food and a home to the birds is the same Father who promises to meet your needs. He is intimately involved in your daily affairs, and he wants you to trust that he is going to take care of you.

Begin to see yourself as one who is loved by a gracious, forgiving, interested Father. You are not alone. You are loved.

When you cry out, the Father's arms are there to make sure you don't fall. You may feel like you're falling, but you're not. You are valuable to the Father and he wants to be involved in your daily life. Will you let him? Or will you cling to your tree in the margins?

HE WANTS TO BE WITH YOU

When I was a kid I had a friend whose dad lived on the East Coast. My friend was growing up in California, thousands of miles away from his father. Even if he wanted to be with his dad, he couldn't. He didn't have access to him. They saw each other once or twice a year and they had a pretty good time together, but what Shawn wanted most was daily access to his dad.

We often think of God that way. *The Father lives in heaven, not here. I live in this broken world and I fight a battle with sin every day, and my Father doesn't know what I'm dealing with.* That is a lie. Ephesians 2:18 says that we have been given access to the Father through Jesus. He purchased us from slavery to sin to bring us back to our Father. The incredible reality is, our Father—the King!—wants to be with us, to talk with us, to share our joys and sorrows. Jesus is calling us out of the margins, inviting us to follow him into the greatest life there is. And what we give up in leaving the margins will seem like nothing in light of the tremendous gain of our Father's love.

This truth sets me free when I let it. I have the choice to believe, and I have to choose to believe I am set free. At first it seemed too good to be true. I would bombard myself with reasons the Father should not love me. *I am too sinful,* I would tell myself. Then Jesus would remind me that my Father is a gracious forgiver and his Son's death is sufficient for my sin. *But I don't deserve it,* I would remind myself, certain that the margins would be my home forever. But Jesus said, "You are valuable to your Father, and grace is all about getting what you don't deserve."

It's still hard to believe that I don't have to earn this love. But that's the beauty of the Father's heart.

BECOMING
THE CHILD

When you wander around the margins and you meet people and hear their stories, you often hear about a childhood that was lost. Obviously, that's not the case for everyone; some people cherish their childhood recollections. But for many, their childhood is a vague, distant memory they would just as soon forget. Maybe their past is painful or traumatic or marked by upheaval, but somewhere along the line innocence was lost. And they tried to forget.

We've created entire generations of lost children. For years now, one out of two marriages has ended in divorce, wreaking havoc on what it means to be a child. When your mom and dad get divorced, you deal with things like loss and grief and abandonment. You have to grow up pretty quickly to handle adult kinds of pain.

We hear all the time in the media that we are over-populating the earth—in other words, we're having too many kids. In this world, a child is thought of more as a problem than as a gift. Over a million children every year are aborted, speaking clearly to our culture's attitude toward children: They are disposable.

This throwaway attitude does nothing to slow the devaluing of innocence. And so second-grade kids are listening to music and engaging in conversation that is way too adult for them. Within a couple of years, many are smoking, drinking, or using drugs, and some are experimenting with sexual behavior.

Jesus invites us to reimagine life as a child of God. But when so many have lost their innocence so early, we have to ask, What does it mean to be a child? How do we recover that which has been lost?

In Matthew 18, Jesus' disciples ask a more adult question: "Who is the greatest in the kingdom of heaven?" The question comes from pressures similar to those you and I face in the world we live in. The question is one of power, prestige, and position. Who among us will be the best and most successful? What do we have to do to earn first place in your kingdom?

Jesus' answer must stagger them. He calls over a small boy (perhaps). The child wanders over as his mom pushes him toward Jesus. Then Jesus lays a hand on his shoulder and says to his followers, "Unless you *change* and become like little children, you will never enter the kingdom of heaven."

Huh? What is he talking about? These are full-grown men! What is he asking of them? What is he asking of *us*? Does he expect us to cry when we don't get our way? Does he want us to play Rock Paper Scissors to make business decisions? What is Jesus getting at?

To really understand what Jesus means by this command, we need to recapture what it means to be a child. This is not an invitation to become childish; it is an invitation to be transformed, to rediscover the beautiful qualities of being a child.

WALKING IN WONDER

I have four kids and they are full of the wonder of bugs and insects. They're full of wonder of the sky and the weather. It doesn't take much to draw them into a place of awe at the world around them.

My son Bryce wants to be a zookeeper when he gets older. (I haven't told him the part about cleaning out the cages yet.) He loves animals. When we went to the beach one summer, we had to take his hermit crabs with us. He has names for them—Spike, See-Through, Baseball, and Fire, all named for the unique features of their shells. Each morning we hiked down to the beach to play in the tide pools, and Bryce would happily tote his bucket carrying the hermit crabs. He would carefully place the hermit crabs in the tide pools so they could walk around and get their exercise. While they were playing, Bryce collected sand dollars and starfish. He is enamored with God's creation. It isn't a stretch for him to walk in wonder.

I, on the other hand, have to work at it. I didn't see the need to bring the hermit crabs with us on vacation, let alone to the beach. I couldn't understand why, after seeing one starfish, we had to look at all the others (and there were hundreds of them).

The difference between the two of us? Bryce walks in the wonder of creation before God, and I am under the illusion that I have grown beyond such simple things. But in Jesus' economy, Bryce gets first place in the kingdom. He is living life as a child of God. I'm busy serving God as a pastor, but I am missing the party. Jesus warns me to get off that road as quickly as possible because I am missing the kingdom.

So I'm training myself to learn from Bryce, to see what he is seeing. To see the creativity of our God who has made amazing creatures for Bryce to enjoy. To touch and feel this creation, to pick it up and examine it. To be fully alive to God's wonder.

FREEDOM TO PLAY

We live in the Pacific Northwest, so our swimming pool is of use to us only two months out of the year; then it starts to rain again and the pool returns to duty as a duck pond. But during those two months our twins, Josh and Kaylee, will play in that pool for hours at a time. They invent games; they try to hear each other talk underwater; they throw things in and dive down to get them. They tolerate less-than-warm water for hours on end, day after day. Why do they do it? Because the heart of a child loves to play.

Meanwhile, I'm busy cleaning the pool, checking

the chlorine and pH levels, and adding chemicals to get the water just right. To me the pool is a project, not a playground. I spend ten times as many hours working on the pool as I do swimming in it. My kids look at me cross-eyed. *What's wrong with Dad?* Then I jump in and do cannonballs and engage my kids in water fights and I remember what the pool is for.

Jesus keeps inviting me to rest in his control and let him worry about the details. He calls me to enjoy the same freedom to play that my children still possess.

FREEDOM TO CREATE

From modeling clay to finger paints to elaborately imaginative games, kids love to create. Some grow out of it and let technology dictate to them what fun is. But the minute you unplug the computer or turn off the TV, they quickly find the creative heart again.

We have a lot of artists in our community of faith, wonderful people who have not lost this freedom. One such artist is Anneli. She painted the picture on the cover of this book onstage during one of our worship services. Anneli told me how she learned that having the heart of a child was a crucial piece of Jesus' calling her to be an artist. She took on a new understanding of what it means to walk in wonder when she began to reimagine herself as a beloved child of God.

Anneli sees the colors that Jesus made as incredible instruments he is telling her to play with. As she paints for us during worship, you can see her sense of childlike freedom. The end result is an awe-inspiring work of art that draws us all into the heart of Jesus. But without that freedom of a child to create, she would simply use God's colors to paint a picture of her own making. Instead, she allows the Spirit of God to speak through her as she walks in the wonder of a childlike relationship.

LIVING LIFE UNASHAMED

Children have this beautiful lack of shame. Every night after my little boys, who are four and five, get out of the bathtub, they come streaking through the house, totally naked, screaming and having fun. There will come a time when they will realize they should cover themselves up, as Adam and Eve covered themselves in the Garden, their innocence lost. But for now my boys have an innate sense that they are, in fact, acceptable.

I find that many high school and college kids and even adults are ashamed of their bodies, ashamed of their physical appearance, because life has taught them that you have to *prove* yourself to be acceptable. From stick-figure fashion models to sculpted celebrities strutting their stuff on the red carpet, our culture teaches us that there is a right way to look and a wrong way to look. It's no wonder we're consumed with our appearance. *My nose is too big. My hair is too curly. My stomach is too fat.* We dip our big toe in the sea of narcissism and we end up falling in.

If you go about concerned with what others think of how you look, you're stuck in the margins. Yes, you need to care for the body God has given you; in fact, exercise and diet can be a way of worshiping him. But even the shapeliest body won't make you more acceptable before God. As our culture screams at you to change your appearance, listen closely for the still, small voice of Jesus. He is inviting you to live life unashamed of how he created you, like a child who isn't caught up in the latest trends but happily worships using his entire body.

Children take joy in being who they are.

Perhaps the most beautiful aspect of kids is that they are spiritually unashamed—trust in God is a natural thing for them. My four-year-old, Bryce, is our resident theologian. He prayed one night, "Jesus, thank you for dying to take away my sins, and thank you that you give them back." Children are not afraid of being found out. And they are not ashamed of their thoughts about God. Walk into a children's class at church and you will find kids speaking their minds, willingly sharing questions they have about God. "Why did God take my dog to heaven?" The kinds of questions that can throw children's ministry workers into a theological panic.

But in adult classes you will find most grown-ups shudder at the thought of even praying out loud in public. Why? Because adults tend to be spiritually ashamed. Children are not. Somewhere along the line we bought into the lie that we should be ashamed before God. But the cross declares to us that God is good and that we are accepted because Jesus' death was sufficient to cover our shame.

Jesus is inviting you to see yourself as *he* sees you, not what our culture says you are or are not. He wants you to recognize your eternal status and accept yourself as a uniquely created child of the Most High God.

LEARNING TO TRUST

Growing up teaches you pretty quickly that people are going to let you down. Think back on your own life. When did you start to mistrust others? We react to a broken trust with an inner vow that we may not even articulate to ourselves, but it is there. We tell ourselves, *I will never trust anyone again because I am tired of being let down.* That kind of thinking is a one-way trip to the margins of life. People *will* let you down, but Jesus' answer is always to forgive. But then we tend to project our betrayals onto Jesus as well. In the margins, people often don't trust Jesus; they are skeptical that he is indeed good and that his promises can be trusted.

Jesus invites us to come to him with a childlike trust, but in the name of maturity, we think Jesus is asking us to check our brains at the door. That is not what he's saying. Still, we keep our hearts at a distance while running through a checklist of logic and reason to see if this Jesus can be trusted. The danger when

you posture yourself like this is that Jesus can never
get to your heart.

At some point, we must come to the place where
we are willing to say, *Jesus, I love you, and I am trusting
you with my life and taking you at your word.* Then our
hearts will connect with his and we can begin to
reimagine life in him.

INNOCENCE RESTORED

My son Josh and I were watching the Super Bowl
halftime show when Janet Jackson had her
"wardrobe malfunction." Josh was eleven at the
time. We were hanging out and pigging out and
doing the Super Bowl party thing when Janet comes
on and reveals herself to the nation. My son just
looked at me with a deer-in-the-headlights stare. He
was confused. I was confused. Then the commer-
cials come on and I have to explain to him what
erectile dysfunction is.

Even as we're doing something that should be
innocent fun, like watching a football game, our fallen
culture is devouring the innocent. From peek-a-boo
halftime shows to highly publicized court battles to
keep Internet porn easily accessible, our culture mocks
childhood innocence. Yet there remains some rudi-
mentary assumption, even in this day and age, that
children should not be exposed to certain things. And
so we develop weak moviegoing guidelines to designate
what children can see and when they can see it. The

Motion Picture Association of America (MPAA) has determined that when children are thirteen they are ready to view love scenes with partial nudity and hear the F-bomb mixed in with really coarse humor. *Why? Who said they were ready?*

If you're thirteen, our culture is ready to project images of sin onto the screen of your mind that will be difficult to erase. Why? Because they want to make a buck! Today's culture isn't much different from the cultures that have gone before us; it's just quicker and more tech-savvy.

Jesus says that the primary objective of Satan is to kill, steal, and destroy. In short, he is out to steal our innocence. When innocence is gone, a deep wound is inflicted on the soul—a wound that consigns us to the spiritual margins. Many people even come to delight in that which is evil. They grow accustomed to sin and the brokenness of our culture and are entertained by it. It's tough to reimagine life as a child of God when you spend your leisure time and money on things that harm your soul.

When the show *Cops* arrived on television, it was an immediate hit. People loved to watch other people getting busted in their sin. I remember the last time I watched the show. The cops were on a drug raid and had just broken into a house. They stormed the place, running from room to room, their weapons drawn. They threw a man to the ground and cuffed him. Then they hauled out a woman who went screaming and kicking and cussing.

Then the camera panned down to show us a two-year-old girl. She was crying and scared because her mommy had just been arrested. This two-year-old girl had just lost her innocence. And millions of viewers, including me, were being entertained by it. Who is the guiltiest? The parents? The cops? The producers? Or the viewers who keep tuning in?

I'm not attempting to answer the ethical questions of the day, but I am saying that when the loss of innocence constitutes entertainment, something's wrong.

The only way out of the margins is to agree with Jesus that we need to change, that we need to become like an innocent child. But first we must recognize that it's only in him that such change can take place. He is inviting you now to reimagine life in him with the innocence of a child. You may have been exposed to sin and engaged in sin that has left deep imprints on your life. Jesus alone has the power to restore you to walk in innocence. When his blood was shed on the cross, he paid for all the sin you have seen and taken part in. Let him change you.

A HUMBLING EXPERIENCE

Jesus explains in very practical terms what it means to change and become childlike. He tells us, "Whoever humbles himself like this child is the greatest in the kingdom" (Matthew 18:4). When it comes to deep inner transformation that will bring us out of the margins, we are to humbly choose to obey Jesus, to put ourselves under his love and protection and authority.

What does this mean for you? You must make four choices daily until you learn to live like a child of God. It may take six weeks or it may take six years, but do not give up.

Living like a child of God first means you must choose to walk in the wonder of worship. Daily choose to see the world around you with wonder and awe, just as a young child does.

The second choice you must make is to trust Jesus with a childlike faith. The Father wants to lavish his love on you in Jesus. Don't remain hiding in the margins, trying to keep God from letting you down. He won't, by the way! But you must choose to trust him.

The third choice you must make daily is to live unashamed before Jesus, believing that his blood was sufficient to forgive you and heal you of those things that name you as flawed. You are rightfully his, and you can stand before him unashamed, for he has chosen you. Don't hide from him in the darkness and isolation of the margins. Live before him in his perfect love like a joyful child.

The fourth and final choice you must make to humble yourself as a child is to walk in innocence. Romans 16:19 tells us "to be wise about what is good, and innocent about what is evil." That means to let God, and not the entertainment industry, determine what is acceptable for you to participate in. Spend your energy each day finding out what Jesus says is good and give yourself to that, while you avoid that which is evil. If you are unsure where the line is, just think of that child in Jesus' arms. Would it be good for him to participate in it?

You may think this is going overboard, but trust me as one who carries deep scars from lost innocence: Being childlike is better than being scarred. Humble yourself and choose his way. Let yourself be changed by the love of Jesus.

RELOCATION

One of the places where Jesus calls us to reimagine life is in the home. For some, home is a place that was safe and warm and filled with fond memories. For others, home is a dysfunctional place where individuals fought for independence from one another. In our cultural moment the meaning of home has become so fractured from the symbolism of family that *home* can only concretely refer to a house that people live in. When reduced to the lowest common denominator, *home* is a sterile, lifeless place.

When you grow up in a home where individuals are doing little more than sharing space, you miss out on key relationships that create a sense of security and belonging. And you're left with a homeless heart. The margins are full of people for whom the idea of home is a fuzzy one.

Cable television offers channels that still portray home as a place where happy families gathered together in simpler times to live out the American dream. I'm sure people must be watching these reruns of *Little House on the Prairie* and *Leave It to Beaver,* but there is a clear disconnect between these classic programs and real life.

Once upon a time a TV network could build a new series around the idea of home as a place of relational belonging in the belief they were providing entertainment that most people could connect with. Today such shows no longer speak for the consensus. We cannot assume that *home* in our society describes a husband and wife and their children, nor even in more general terms, a place of support and safety within the bounds of loving relationship. Today many of us live hundreds or even thousands of miles from the place where we grew up. Half of us have parents who have been divorced. So the rallying point of today's programming is not the home but the individual and his or her friends, as in the long-running sitcom of the same name.

The reason that our TV shows don't depict modern-day *Leave It to Beaver* homes is because those homes no longer exist. Did anyone reading this book come home to find Mom in a prom dress, vacuuming with one hand and pulling warm cookies out of the oven with the other, while Dad trimmed the hedges in his three-piece suit? It is no longer safe to assume that our homes have a husband and wife in them. It is no longer safe to assume that loving relationships describe the environment of our homes. The only thing we can assume is that we all came from some kind of home and many of us don't want to go back to it.

Yet deep within our souls there is a longing for home.

We can't really put words to it, but we know it's there. This longing does not betray us—it is telling us something. It's telling us that home is not just an outdated idea but is the way things *should* be.

Home is meant to be a place of belonging where we are welcomed to the table by people who are happy we are there. There are dreams being shared and realized. There is celebration as people grow and accomplish. There are hugs and tears when dreams are dashed and life is challenging. At home, we belong and we are not alone.

HOME IS MORE THAN A HOUSE

A few years ago I spoke at a friend's church in the Bahamas. The home where I stayed was an amazing place, a massive house located on an inlet about a hundred yards from the ocean. Each morning I looked out my bedroom window and soaked it all in—the tropical sun, the ocean breeze, the white beaches, the host family's fifty-foot yacht docked next to their twenty-foot fishing boat. It was paradise.

I was there for a week, but it only took a few hours to get that feeling deep in my stomach—the sick feeling of missing home. *Why?* Was I nuts? I was in paradise! Why in the world would I be missing my much smaller and incredibly less impressive house in rainy Oregon?

The answer is simple: I missed my wife and children. I missed the core relationships of my life, the relationships that define home for me. I would gladly trade houses, but when it comes to being away from my family, a week is too long to be gone. Weird? Not really.

Home is about the relationships, not the roof.

But if we peer through the windows of an average American home today, is that what we will see? There is a seven-year-old playing his Xbox. He's been there since he got home from school almost three hours ago. His twelve-year-old sister is on the phone, talking to her friend. She keeps an eye on her brother after school until Mom gets home from work. Dad lives in another state with their stepmother and her kids. Mom works a lot just to make it financially. She gets home at around 6:30. Tonight she has a date after work, so the kids are on their own for dinner. There are plenty of things in the freezer that they can pop into the microwave.

Mom's not to blame. She has a lot on her plate. She really wants to marry again, if only because she doesn't think she can keep up this pace. She wants to be home for her kids, but that's not the hand she's been dealt. The kids are good kids. They do well in school and have friends. They miss their dad but get to spend a few weekends a year with him, plus two weeks in the summer.

The boy doesn't feel much one way or another about the whole thing. He just pours himself into video games and watches a lot of TV. When Mom comes home, she helps him with his homework and he catches a quick shower and heads to bed. He doesn't really know his grandparents; they live in a different state and he only sees them at Christmas every other year.

His sister doesn't care much about home anymore. She hates watching her little brother; she wants to be free to go out with her friends. Boys are her new favorite topic of conversation, but she hides that fact that she has a boyfriend from her mom. To her, home is just a place where you eat, sleep, and get dressed in the morning. Life is out *there* and she can't wait to go after it.

Notice as we look through this window that the people inside the home are each focused on their individual lives without any deep relational connection to the others. They are individuals who make up a whole, but the whole has little meaning. For them, home is a building, not relationships.

Was this true for you, that home was little more than a house or an apartment? A place where you slept and ate your meals? Jesus wants to redeem the picture of home you have in your mind. He wants to heal your experience, if needed, and redefine it for you. Then he wants you to reimagine yourself at home in God. But how?

HOME AS A PICTURE OF HEAVEN

When a person dies, you may hear his friends say, "He went home," or "She's in a better place now, at home with the Lord." What does that mean? Does that mean he is being greeted by June Cleaver with freshly-baked cookies? Does it mean that she's locking herself in her room while her parents are fighting? What does it mean to think of heaven as home?

In 2 Corinthians 5:8, the apostle Paul says that he would rather be absent from his body and be at home with the Lord. Paul uses the idea of home to illustrate that heaven is a place of belonging with Jesus. It is a place where you fit in. Heaven is the place where followers of Christ will find ultimate belonging, acceptance, and security. Paul wants to be in the presence of Jesus and the Father. Why? Because it is the place where his relationship with Jesus will be fully realized. That relationship with the Father, Son, and Spirit is what makes it home.

When I used to think of heaven, I had trouble connecting to it. From everything I had heard, it didn't seem like a place where I would be comfortable. When I pictured God there with the angels and all the saints, I remember thinking I would feel like the odd man out. I could picture everyone looking at me and whispering, "How did he get in here?"

To my thinking, heaven was a place for people who were not like me.

The Bible teaches us that just the opposite is true. When we come to believe in Jesus, he changes our souls and makes us fit for heaven. It's not something that we can do in our power, but instead is a miracle that Jesus does in us. When the day comes for me to walk into heaven, Paul says, it will be a homecoming.

I won't feel like the odd man out; rather, it will be like walking into my own home. I will be welcomed in as a child who has been away. Jesus will be waiting there and he'll be really stoked to see me. And there will be a place for you, too—there is a place in his home for every believer. You and I won't feel like invited guests.

We will feel at home.

When we are finally with Jesus, we will never have known greater peace. We will be filled with the security and love that only Christ can offer. We will not enter into his home and feel as if we have to compete for his attention. We will not feel as if we are being compared to others or spend eternity trying to measure up. In heaven you can be yourself and fit in just fine. We will fit in because Christ's redemption has made us fit in. Whether we have come from the best earthly homes or the worst, we will share the same sense of awe as we walk into this place of unlimited belonging. Every one of us will be blown away as we finally realize the true meaning of what it is to be home.

But what about now?

What happens in the meantime? Our experience of home should have pointed us to the reality of heaven, but sin has left its destructive marks all over the word *home*. So what can we do to change our perception of home? Jesus answers these questions for us.

In John 14:23, he teaches that those who obey him and love him will experience the intimacy of our heavenly home here and now. He says, "If anyone loves me, he will obey my teaching. My Father will love

him, and we will come to him and make our home
with him." The word he uses for "home" literally
means the place where one resides or dwells. In this
monumental statement, Jesus replaces the location of
home from a building to the inner life of the believer,
because that is where our relationship with God is
being realized. In other words, Jesus and the Father will
set up home in the hearts of those who trust him.

Jesus clearly states the requirements for his and the
Father's moving in. He tells us that we need to love
him and obey his teaching. That is the definition of a
Christ-follower: someone who loves Jesus and is trying
to live life as he has defined it for us.

NON-RELATIONAL OBEDIENCE AND DISOBEDIENT LOVE

Honestly, American Christians have struggled with
this. We tend to fall into one of two camps: non-
relational obedience and disobedient love. In the
first camp we find people who do all the right
things but for the wrong reasons. They go to
church, read their Bible, and put little fish on their
bumpers. But when you look closer at their hearts'
motives, you don't find relationship at the core; you
find religion. These people are trying to *earn* their
way to God by showing him that they are good
enough. These people are invariably tired because
they are trying to do something that is impossible—
we can never be good enough; that is why the cross

is there. Such people look good on the outside, but inside they are homeless.

The other camp is disobedient love. These are people who claim to love Jesus but have no intention of submitting their lives to his will or trying to live as he did. They compromise their souls with sin. They're determined to live how they want to live, even when Jesus says they're headed in the wrong direction. "I love Jesus," they exclaim, "but I am not giving up sex with my girlfriend," or "I am not going to quit cheating on my taxes."

The people in both of these camps are homeless. They refuse to love Jesus *and* obey him. But God is looking to set up home in people who choose to run the course of life that Jesus has set out for us.

UNCONDITIONAL ACCEPTANCE

One of the reasons many of us fall into the camp of non-relational obedience is that deep down we really don't believe that we are accepted by God. Life in the margins has taught us that we must prove ourselves worthy of acceptance. Unfortunately, the acceptance that the culture offers is always conditional.

But what about people who can't perform? There are countless men and women who are marginalized by their handicaps, whether mental or physical. It may be that they were born with a low IQ or some physical defect that makes it impossible for a person to be successful in our culture's eyes. They are, however, fully capable of receiving love.

There is a ministry called L'Arche where mentally handicapped people live in community. In this place there is unconditional acceptance. In more than one hundred and twenty communities around the world, L'Arche residents are accepted for who they are, not what they can do. They, in turn, teach others what true acceptance is, despite being unable to reach the performance bar set by our culture.

That is what being at home in God is like—it is a place of unconditional acceptance. You are accepted because of what Christ has done for you, not because of what you can do for Christ. When we compare ourselves to God, who is perfect, we can see that the picture of L'Arche is not a stretch. We don't come with a lot to offer him, from a performance standpoint. But the desire of Jesus is not that you perform. It is simply that you receive the love he has for you and respond by loving him in return. Jesus wants you to be at home in God and rest in the acceptance he has already purchased for you with his blood.

UNSHAKEABLE SECURITY

I love coming home. It is the one place where I can truly be me. If my hair is a mess, my kids don't look at me like I'm a stranger. When I sit on the couch and put my feet up and my children climb onto my lap, I experience belonging. So many of us grew up without the freedom to be who we are, and so many still live in the margins, trying to fit in. They feel like visitors living out of a relational suitcase, never feeling like they can fully unpack and decorate their room.

When we don't feel like we belong and are never sure if we're good enough, then we become wrought with insecurity. And we try to make up for it in unhealthy ways. I talked with one margin-dweller who spoke of how her mom and dad would split up and get back together over and over, until they finally were divorced. She never knew coming home from school whether Dad would be living there or not. Every time her parents argued, she feared that Dad would be packing his bags and leaving.

I love it when God says, "Never will I leave you; never will I forsake you" (Hebrews 13:5). God will never leave the home he is creating in your heart. You don't have to worry about him packing his bags and taking off. So rest in the security of your relationship with him. Even sin won't send him packing, because if we confess our sins he will forgive us and purify us. He cleans up our heart to make it fit for him to dwell in.

Jesus wants you to feel secure, to be fully at home in God. You belong with him. You don't have to leave your suitcase packed. You can put on your pajamas and climb up next to him and relax in his presence. If you think this is too good to be true, it's probably because you are living in one of the two extremes of non-relational obedience or disobedient love wracked with unbelief. But Jesus has redeemed you from that, and he is inviting you to reimagine.

When I was growing up we had the best family

gatherings. Come birthdays or New Year's Eve or Christmas, you could count on a big party. Sometimes as many as fifty people would show up at Grandma and Grandpa's house. The food was abundant, the margaritas were made by Gramps, and people had the best time. If you looked around the room you would find that everyone there was there because of Grandma and Grandpa. We were all relationally connected to them, and we were living it up because we belonged. I know that heaven will be even better than those times, but the memories help paint a picture for me of what heaven will be like. A celebration in heaven with brothers and sisters who are all at home, belonging, accepted, and secure because of their relationship with God. The Father, Son, and Spirit are throwing the greatest party ever, and all the drinks are on them.

A WELCOME GUEST?

So how do you feel about God moving in? If you are a Christ-follower, he already has. Imagine you were to get a phone call from someone who tells you that they just got into town and need to stay with you for a few months while they get on their feet. How do you feel inside? It really depends on who it is, doesn't it? If it's some long-lost cousin you don't know, you probably won't be real excited. If it's your fiancé and you're to be married in the morning, you'll probably be pretty excited. When God moves in, we should be extraordinarily excited. The One who loves you more than anyone else does is coming into your life to stay. It's just the beginning of a life together that will culminate when you see him face-to-face.

Have you ever gone to someone's house and got the feeling they didn't want you there? That's awkward. You walk in expecting to be greeted warmly, but you get the cold shoulder. The host doesn't really pay attention to you. They go off to another room, doing whatever, while you stand in the entryway, holding your coat and wondering if you should leave.

Is God a welcome guest in your life?

Is he sitting in the hallway, wondering if you're going to invite him in or kick him out? Or are you welcoming him to stay and feel free to go wherever he wants? Does he have access to all the rooms in your life?

When God moves in, it is his intention that we enter fully into the depths of his love for us. We belong with him and that makes all the difference in the here and now. We will still experience tough times, but nothing can separate us from his love, where we find the truest sense of *home*. It is not a building; it is a deeply personal, spiritual relationship.

Reimagine!

DYING IN THE DESERT OF SELF

We are lonely people, those of us who live in the margins. Inside each of us is the longing to belong, but we find it hard to engage in those relationships that could bring us into community. We don't necessarily have the relational tools to enter into authentic community, even if we could find people who would accept us for who we are.

We come by it rightly, this need to be in relationship. When God created the first man, Adam, he said it was not good for the man to be alone. So he created Eve to be the man's wife. The first marriage gives us insight into human composition: We all need to belong.

Today we see people connected in all kinds of ways, all stemming from the longing to belong. Our world is getting smaller. Most of us can know what is going on anywhere else in the world at a moment's notice. We can communicate almost instantaneously via phone and e-mail with people in the most remote countries. The movies and TV shows that are popular in America soon become popular around the globe.

I have two good friends who grew up in Ireland. I was visiting there for a few weeks when we first met. While talking we soon realized that we shared many of the same interests. We had grown up watching the same movies. They knew where Yellowstone National Park was because of Yogi Bear (who lived in the fictional Jellystone). We sang U2 songs together. We discovered that we spoke a common language—the language of popular culture.

Of course, I probably had the same things in common with many other Irish people. But there was something more that connected the three of us, something that would make us good friends, lasting friends. There was a bigger story that ran through all three of our lives: the Christ story.

We had Christ in common.

Our common experience of his love and grace is the thing that has kept our hearts knit together. Culture could not take us there. Culture gave us affinity; Christ gave us a common unity. We were all three united in Christ.

The fact is, culture cannot offer us real community. It offers us entertainment. It offers us material things. But it can't offer us what we deeply long for—relationship. Even though billions of people are connected by common points of cultural reference, there is still tremendous loneliness. We spend our lives in chat rooms with made-up names and tell people things about ourselves that are not true. We find a sense of shared identity in a favorite sports team or a musician that we both like. That is not community; it is affinity. We climb into our beds at night insecure because no one really knows us. We don't usually lie there awake, going over it in our minds. No, it's more like static, white noise in the back of our hearts. It's always buzzing at us, but we tune it out.

What about the church? Can't we find community there? The relationship Jesus has brought us into with the Father is supposed to overflow into our relationships with one another.

We're supposed to be a family. Brothers and sisters in Christ.

Tragically, for most of us the church is not a place where we feel we can be authentic. *After all, what if somebody there should find out that I'm struggling with sin, that I'm not living the victorious Christian life?* So we all put on masks and cover up what's really going on. And our sin grows in isolation.

Isolation is the garden of the devil. If he can convince you not to be real with people and shame you into thinking that you're the only one who thinks like that or has failed, he can get you off to the sidelines and keep you there. Your heart will begin to shrivel up and your faith will be deeply challenged. That is why the margins are so prevalent in the church. Somewhere along the line we bought into the world's understanding of how we're supposed to do life. We started keeping up appearances, and in that place we were robbed of the communal faith that Jesus died to give us.

You and I were never called to live this Christian life alone. Community is central to being a Christ-follower, and it's vital to reimagining life in Jesus. Satan can have his way with believers as long as they're stuck in the margins, and so he has taught us to believe any number of lies.

THE LIE OF INDIVIDUALISM

The lie of individualism is a huge lie we've bought into here in America. This began a few hundred years ago with the onset of modernity. It essentially says that all understanding begins with me—*I am the center of my universe. I can make something of myself. I can be a self-made person. I will win.* When the world is implicitly about me then it cannot be about *you*, at least not in my thinking.

This lie flies in the face of Christ's example. Remember Peter, the businessman we met back in chapter 1? Here's a guy who has made it. He has the house, the car, the wife, and the cash. But he is still lonely. Why? Because he is stuck in the margins of individualism. He believes that he's traveling on a one-lane road and the most important use of his resources is to fill his lane with whatever makes him happy.

The path of individualism breeds a self-centeredness

that we cannot shake. Even in our best deeds, we still look for the payoff to us.

What's in it for me?

The culture we live in is about *our* making it for *our* glory. Plain and simple. The result of this is that people fail to engage in deep relationships. There are few places where they are really known, not even in their own marriages and families. Everyone is too busy looking out for themselves.

This same individualism has crept into the church with tragic results. These days we like to say that our faith is "a private matter." *It's just about me and Jesus. Get out of my lane.* This has created a church culture that personalizes faith to the detriment of community. We've bought into the lie that if we're to connect people to God we must first meet their individualistic needs. On Sunday when a family arrives at church, we send their kids off to age-specific classes, while the wife goes to a class for women her age and the husband attends a class for men. When they get back to the car they seldom talk about what they experienced. Why? Because there is an unspoken rule: *This is my lane and you don't get to tell me what to do or believe. Worry about your own lane. Mine is fine.*

By segmenting everyone into age-specific classes or special interest groups, we reinforce the lie of individualism. We implicitly teach that the church is there to meet the individual's needs. We treat them like spectators in the process, not key participants.

This approach puts the church in the position of selling Jesus—trying to get you to come by catering to your specific needs.

If faith is truly a private matter, then the only thing Christians have in common is a regular event called church, and there is no authentic relationship with one another in Christ. The shame of spiritual isolation is compounded when we realize that even at church no one knows who we really are. I talked with one person who told me that if anyone at church really knew who she was, the doubts and struggles she faced, they simply would not accept her. That floats over her head like a cartoon thought-bubble in a comic strip. It forces her to smile at church and tell everyone how great she is doing. The irony is, everyone there has the same bubble over their head and is thinking the same thing. And our enemy Satan has a field day.

Jesus and the New Testament writers tell us that we *need* each other. We need each other to help us develop into all that God intends for us to become. In Galatians 5:13, we are told to use the freedom that Christ purchased for us not to keep sinning and abuse his grace, but to serve one another. You and I now exist for *other* people. We are to shift our focus away from ourselves and onto others, to look for ways to love and take care of other people. Christ set us free so we could leave our lanes and look out for one other.

People in prison have to look out for themselves.

There, selfishness is at the very core of survival. Fights break out over food and cigarettes, because inmates have nothing and must take what they can for themselves. But we are not in prison; we have been set free by Jesus. So why do we insist on using our freedom for self-gain and not to help others?

In the world's economy, life is not much different from prison—we're all fighting to get what we can out of life. But the church is not supposed to mimic our culture or the life of those who are not free. Instead, it is meant to be a place where people are so grateful that Jesus has given his life for their sin that they are looking for a chance to mimic him by serving others. We are to serve one another and complement one another's gifts for the common purpose of representing Christ to our world.

Jesus invites you to reimagine life as a key participant in his family. The ball is in your court.

THE LIE OF AUTONOMY

The crippling lie of self-sufficiency led to the first sin, when Satan convinced Adam and Eve that they didn't need God. This lie has since been woven into the fabric of our culture and the church: *I don't need anyone to tell me what to do. I can take care of myself. I am perfectly capable of making my own decisions.* And so we strive for autonomy, for independence, but when a person finally achieves it he dies inside.

That's because we were never meant to take care of ourselves. Each of us was created to be dependent—on God and on one another.

We are wired for community. Literally. Each of us has a belly button. Some are outies, some are innies, some are pierced. But we all carry this unmistakable sign that shows we were at one time physically connected to our mothers. Life begins for every human in utter dependence on another. But as we grow, our culture slowly sucks us into believing that we will truly be liberated only when we no longer need to depend on someone else. Yet in our liberation we find oppression—we fight for autonomy only to end up lonely, tired, and struggling.

We've all met someone who is difficult to work with. You know the type: *It's either my way or the highway.* You can't get very far with these people. They're autonomous. But self-sufficiency is also more subtle than that. It creeps into our way of thinking. We pass judgment on others who are not like us. We find it hard to trust God and almost impossible to trust other people. We are reluctant to expose our true selves, our thoughts, our emotions. We hold our cards close to the vest. We try to be our own god, and we wear ourselves out trying to control our own universe. And all the time we still have the need to belong. So we try to fill our longing with sin and end up more broken than when we started.

Some of us try to belong and be autonomous at the same time, but it doesn't work. You often see this in the church. If we don't like what the pastor says, we fire him. If we don't like the music, we complain. If the leadership tries to corral us into a small group, we buck even harder. Finally, if our needs aren't being catered to, we leave. We take our money with us and think, *That'll teach them.*

Jesus wants us to reimagine ourselves as participants in his redeemed family. Note that I say *participant*, not *spectator*. But the lie of autonomy tells us that the lack of love in the church is someone else's problem, not mine.

So we sit in the bleachers and watch.

We watch as people are hurting and need a friend. We sit idly by as our leaders try to move people toward community. *It's not my problem that I'm self-sufficient*, we think. Jesus says that's a lie. We belong to one another because we belong to Christ. We need to come down out of the stands and do something for someone.

THE LIE OF AFFINITY

We tend to gravitate to people who are like us. People who look like us, talk like us, make about the same money we do, believe what we believe, and enjoy the same entertainment we do. Is that community? No, that's affinity. *We're alike so we can be friends.* What this really boils down to is self-worship. I like you because you are like me. We share the same tastes. I can hang out with you. We are essentially surrounding ourselves with ourselves, only with different names and faces. We may develop a circle of acquaintances this way, but we won't experience the deeper things that make belonging in community the beautiful, biblical thing that it is.

Tragically, the church has bought into the culture's lie of affinity. We go to churches that are full of people just like us. We don't go to this church because Jesus has redeemed us to belong to one another; we go to this church because the members all belong to the same ethnicity or we listen to the same music or we vote the same way or all of the above. We go to this church because the people are just like us. It doesn't take an act of God to get people to like each other if they are all alike. You can find that in any subculture in America.

To the world, the church looks like just another subculture.

In Ephesians 4:2, the author tells us to be humble and gentle, to be patient, bearing with one another in love. We are called to be humble because, before God, that guy who bugs you is on the same plane you are. You *both* needed Christ to die for you. Jesus doesn't see you as a peer and the other guy as a loser. Jesus invites us to humble ourselves from that pride, to bear with one another in love. I sometimes wish he would have said "tolerate." I can do that. I can put up with someone. That's not what the Bible says, though. The command to bear with one another in love *assumes* that people are going to bug you. This is where the lie of affinity makes it tough.

We're willing to travel next to people driving in their own lanes as long as they are kind of like us. But put me next to people who are nothing like me and I want to steer away from them. Jesus tells me that's destructive to his family. He wants me to get my eyes off myself and onto others and bear with them in love. I need to get to know them beyond their annoying habits and see their heart. Caring for people who are different from me is not the pastor's job or the small-group leader's job. It is my job and your job and we need to do it out of love. That pulls us out of the margins of affinity and into the heart of God's family.

In John 14, Jesus tells us to love one another as he has loved us. If God's family really took this seriously and loved one another as Jesus has loved us, we would see a group of people who forgive each other, people who are devoted to each other, people who respect and care for one another. This would be a family of people who don't judge one another but, rather, encourage one another to live life as Jesus has defined it for us. That kind of love looks really strange in this world. In the same passage, Jesus says that all people will know we are his disciples by our love for one another. In other words, his brand of love is so utterly foreign to this *me-first* world that people will know you are following Christ if you love like that.

The question is simple. Does the love you have for God's family look like the love Jesus has for *you?*

You are a participant. No one is off the hook. When you reimagine yourself as a key player in God's family, you choose to love others instead of waiting for them to love you. You are walking in the messy blessing of community.

THE MESSY BLESSING OF COMMUNITY

The picture of the church in the Bible is a messy one. Why? Because community is messy. The lies our culture wants us to buy into are not new. The church has struggled against them since its birth. The mess happens when people who are not like each other begin to do life together. We soon realize that community requires us to fall at Jesus' feet and beg him for the love it takes to obey the "one another" commands. We find we often have to ask people to forgive us because we have not served and loved them the way Jesus wanted us to.

Imagine you're in a group of people getting together to worship. You are all pretty similar. Then a couple of other Christ-followers walk in. One has come straight out of rehab. He's been strung out on drugs for several years and has just given his life to Jesus. The other guy is a wealthy businessman who has just sold his company for fifty million dollars. How do you suppose your group will respond to these two very different men? Will you kiss up to the guy with cash and try to be polite to the guy who just got off drugs? Or will you avoid the guy with cash (because he probably thinks he's better than you) and cater to the guy who is out of rehab (because you think you're better than him and, therefore, he is safe)? Do you question the one guy's motives and wonder if he will really stay sober? Are you so enamored with the rich guy's lifestyle that you're ready to make him a small-group leader?

Why are we like this? It's because we believe the cultural values our world has taught us and we're reluctant to submit to the messy community that Christ has called us into.

Now imagine that Jesus is in the room.

How does *he* see these men? Jesus knows that they both needed his grace and that he had to die to redeem both of them. Therefore, they are both deserving of surpassing love and devotion from other believers. You need them. They need you. They even need each other. Behind the tattoos and the business suit is the same kind of broken life. That's the great thing about authentic community. It's the real us in loving relationship with other real people, all under the grace of the real and living Christ.

So how do we enter into this messy blessing of community? First, we need to believe that what Jesus says is true. Then we need to quit buying into the individualistic lies of our culture. We need to admit to God that we have been living under the power of these lies and, therefore, have not been living in biblical community.

Then we must reimagine life, picturing this new reality of participating in authentic community. We exist for God and others. Let that be the motto of our lives. Let's not wait for someone else to obey Jesus. Be courageous. Find someone who is not like you—perhaps someone older or younger, richer or poorer—and ask that person to meet with you once a week to talk about life and faith and what Jesus is doing in their life and yours. Be honest with one another. Share your mistakes. Confess your sins to one another. The Bible says this will be a healing time.

You will find that Jesus is in the midst of that kind of community. Will you leave your one-lane life to love your brothers and sisters?

WHAT IF MY CHUTE DOESN'T OPEN?

Perhaps by now you are gaining hope. Hope that you can leave the margins. Hope that Jesus' invitation to reimagine life is real. You want to believe. But you may be thinking, *Don't I have to pull this off on my own? If Jesus is in heaven and I am stuck down here trying to escape the margins of life, then how can I even begin to connect with him?* Those are legitimate feelings and great questions. Let me try to answer by sharing my own story of how I came to daily experience Jesus and his invitation to reimagine life in his unending presence.

After I first decided to follow Christ, I was lonely. *Depressed* may be a better term. I didn't hang out much with my old friends because I was leaving the party scene behind. I didn't connect much with the college kids at church either. We seemed to come from very different worlds—many of them *wished* they knew where the parties were and were bummed that they were never invited. So I was in no-man's-land, and it was a pretty lonely place.

On the other hand, I was super-stoked that Jesus had saved me. I would be close to tears during worship, thinking about how God could love me so much and forgive all the things I had done. I was awed by Jesus' sacrifice. I truly had been given a new life and was very grateful to this very good God. But I had been a social animal; I had always been with people and never really alone. Until now.

So here I was, a new believer in Jesus, sitting at home on Friday night with my parents. They didn't know what to do with that. I hadn't been home on a Friday night since I was fourteen. Now all of a sudden I was going to church on Sundays, reading my Bible through the week, and sitting home with them on weekends. My parents thought I was weird; but I thought so, too, so my feelings weren't hurt. I just hung out with them, watching movies together on our 150-pound 1985 VCR.

I remember talking to Jim about my loneliness. Jim was the pastor in our church who oversaw college- and career-aged people. I met with him once a week or so, and he played a key role in shaping my faith. We became friends and still are. Jim taught me about the Bible and kept tabs on how I was doing. One day he asked how it was going. I said, "Good," meaning I was reading my Bible and not totally blowing it in the area of sin. Then I looked at Jim and said, "I just wish Jesus were here so we could hang out." He looked at me kind of funny. I realize now that one of the great things about new believers is that they ask questions the rest of the church thinks you're not supposed to ask.

Here I was, a new Christ-follower eight weeks old in the faith, and Jesus had made such an impact on my heart that all I really wanted was to hang out with him. But I couldn't. He was in heaven and I was on earth. I had the Bible, of course, and the church to help me. But day in and day out, I was unsure of how to connect with the presence of Jesus.

CONNECTING WITH JESUS

I've since learned there are many ideas about what it means to connect relationally with Jesus. I hope to make it simpler for you than it seemed to me at first. Because I believe that Jesus' promises to us are true and connecting to him is not supposed to be impossible to figure out.

As I look back at the beginning of my faith journey, I remember those first days as a time of incredible learning and tender care from the Spirit of God. I learned a ton about who this Jesus is and how he was affecting my life. As I was reading my Bible I came to this amazing passage:

> "If you love me, you will obey what I command. And I will ask the Father, and he will give you another Counselor to be with you forever—the Spirit of truth. The world cannot accept him, because it neither sees him nor knows him. But you know him, for he lives

with you and will be in you. I will not leave
you as orphans; I will come to you." (John
14:15–18)

These words jumped out at me the first time I
read them. I had been sulking in my loneliness. But
here Jesus tells me that he sent the Spirit of truth, the
Holy Spirit, to come and be my counselor, or helper—
literally, "one who is called to walk alongside." That's
what I needed, someone to walk alongside me and
help me to believe and obey and love. But God was
not just sending me a camp counselor or even an angel
to watch over me—he was sending the third person of
the Godhead, his own Spirit!

Suddenly, I was able to understand the Bible
much more clearly. I could depend on the Holy Spirit
to lead me to the truth, which was good because, not
growing up in a church, I didn't know much about
Jesus and I needed constant help. The truth is, I know
a lot more about Jesus now, but I still need constant
help! And the Holy Spirit still walks alongside me
every day to help me know Jesus better. That's Christ's
promise to you and me: "The Counselor, the Holy
Spirit, whom the Father will send in my name, will
teach you all things and will remind you of everything
I have said to you" (John 14:26).

The days following this revelation were sweet.
I could sense physically that God's Spirit was near.
I would read the Bible and pray and invite the
Spirit to show me how to apply what I was reading to

my life, and he would. God gently corrected me when I sinned, and he would affirm his love for me and his acceptance of me. Eventually, I came to a place where I was no longer lonely and I wasn't depressed anymore. God had pulled me through it. It happened when I realized that this relationship I was enjoying with God, through his Word and his Spirit, was never going away. The daily presence I was experiencing was real, but it was just an appetizer for the presence I will experience one day in heaven when I worship Jesus face-to-face.

BACK TO THE MARGINS

I felt deep joy for the first time and was able to tell God I would go wherever he wanted me to go. I left for Bible college a short time later. From my times of studying and prayer and sensing his Spirit, I knew God was calling me to serve him. But I had no clue how or why or what that might look like. I just loaded up my stuff and headed for Bible college.

Soon after I started attending classes I was feeling overwhelmed and clueless. The truth is, I *was* clueless. The other students were much smarter than I, and most had been following Christ for much longer. Then there were the teachers, who understood Greek and Hebrew and knew the Bible inside and out. I began to doubt whether the presence of God in my life was real. So I studied harder and soon found myself trying to please people instead of God.

People-pleasing is an insidious trap. Satan uses it to steal the beauty of God's presence from our life. In my Bible reading, I was no longer focused on what God was trying to say to me; I was just trying to get it right for the classes I was taking. The voice of the Spirit was growing faint in my life. My whole understanding of grace became twisted as I tried to earn the respect of people, thinking that if they approved of me then God would, too. It wasn't the fault of the church or the school; it was my own distrust in what God was doing and had done in my life.

Had I made it all up? Maybe I hadn't really experienced the presence of God. Maybe it wasn't his voice I had heard. So I wandered back into the desert of loneliness. I left behind the oasis of grace that had saved me to seek after a mirage—the acceptance of those who would be impressed by my knowledge of the Bible. And I did learn the Bible. Soon I could regurgitate all kinds of stuff about the Word and even developed theories on difficult passages. I learned all about ministry and developed a philosophy of ministry that I believed was flawless and would lead to success. And all the while my soul was shrinking.

Now that I was no longer listening for the Spirit, it was up to me to figure out for myself what the Bible meant and how to apply it to my life. As I walked through my day I did not anticipate the presence of the Holy Spirit by my side reminding me of the truth and teaching me how to walk in the way of Jesus. I was back in the margins. Only this time they were religious margins, but margins nonetheless. God had taken the form of an academic institution for me and was waiting to see how I would perform and how much I could know about him before he handed out my grade.

This kind of thinking is all too common in the church today. We attend various conferences, trying to learn all we can, thinking that achieving a certain level of Bible knowledge will persuade God to show up in our life. We put our spiritual leaders on a pedestal, thinking they have it all figured out, but knowing that until we can be like them we're on our own. The tragedy is, we've simply forgotten how to experience the daily presence of Jesus. We long for our first days of faith when his Spirit seemed so near, and yet we've written off those early experiences as merely the enthusiasm of a new believer. Now that we're more "mature" in our faith we know to expect less of our God.

That lie cost my heart a lot.

If you haven't already bought into it, don't! Renounce it or simply declare that it is a lie. God has promised that he has sent his Spirit to be with us as Counselor-Helper living inside us. He *wants* you to experience all the power of the gospel.

I used to worry that if anyone knew how I connected with Jesus they would think I was some kind of TV evangelist and dismiss me as a wacko. I don't fear that now. I don't want to live for people's approval anymore.

Don't get me wrong, I don't like it when people

don't approve of me. I guess what has changed is that I now know that earning the approval of other believers is not the way to connect with Jesus. That's a dead end that leads only to spiritual frustration and isolation. The religious margins.

BEING WITH JESUS

In our journey together we have seen that Jesus redeems us from the power of sin so that we can reimagine life in the fullness of relationship with the Father, Son, and Spirit. Jesus calls us out of the margins and into the fullness of divine love. We have been made acceptable children to live in intimate relationship with God at home in our hearts. Now all we need to do is walk it out. So what does it look like to hang out in the presence of Jesus?

First of all, you need to pay attention. The Spirit of God is living in you and with you, and there are things you can do to cooperate with God in this relationship. Paying attention to him is really the key. Imagine you are married but never pay attention to your spouse. They speak to you but you don't listen. They tell you that you're hurting them with your thoughtlessness, but you are so disconnected that you don't even hear. How intimate would that relationship be? Not very. One of the dangers of religious margins is that they breed an independence that does not allow you to pay attention to the Spirit of God. We end up like that spouse who maybe knows a lot of information about their husband or wife, but does not daily know them in loving relationship.

I hate giving out how-to manuals, especially when it comes to walking with Jesus. In all honesty, I believe the relationship is a bit different for everyone. However, I do believe that there are some important things we need to do to connect daily with the presence of God, which creates an attitude of just *being with*. Not pumping up spiritually to get Jesus to perform for you, but simply *being with* Jesus. I think that's the heart of relationship: I just want to be with Jesus.

When I was stuck in the religious margins, I would read my Bible or pray just to earn Jesus' blessing so he could make me successful in my ministry or my life. I don't feel that way anymore. My friend David Needham once told me, "Rick, remember, Jesus saved you so he could *love* you, not just *use* you!" That has stuck with me.

So here is what I do. As I read the Bible, I pray something like, *God, show me what you want me to learn.* Then I read slowly and I listen. Sometimes I find myself convicted of a sin that is being addressed in the text. If so, I confess it and ask forgiveness. Other times I am reminded of something beautiful about God, so I thank him and tell him how amazing he is to me.

I tell him if I am scared or sad, and I ask Jesus to come into that place with me. At times I hear his voice inside my head. It sounds a lot like my voice but it's usually telling me things I would not make up for myself. He may ask me to pray for someone. The person just comes to mind, so I pray for them. I am simply paying attention and enjoying the presence of Jesus through his Spirit. It's not really that tough, but it does take concentration and focus.

One key is that I don't make this conversation a once-a-day thing. I try to listen to the Spirit and talk to God throughout my day. When I'm talking with someone, I ask God to give me what he wants me to say. I just want to make sure that I'm in an ongoing, moment-by-moment relationship with Jesus. Meanwhile, the Spirit of God is there helping me, reminding me and teaching me.

I wish I could say that I have this down pat. I don't. The thing about religious margins is that you can wander into them and get stuck in their mud without realizing it. If you're not paying attention to what the Spirit is saying to you, then you most likely will stay there and never even know you are stuck.

I don't have to be there, though, and neither do you. As Jesus invites you to reimagine life daily and hang out in his presence, he is simply asking you to pay attention, to believe in and respond to what he is telling you. Simple, but astounding. The beauty of redemption from sin to relationship is ours to experience daily.

Now will you pay attention to this God who has purchased you with the blood of his own Son, who has made you his child and made his home in your heart? If you do, then your journey out of the margins is not dependent on how much you know or what others think; it is all about Jesus' love being poured out into and through your life to others.

It is real. I promise.

POSTCARDS FROM FURTHER DOWN THE ROAD

I met my wife when I was nineteen. I was in college, my
hair was dyed, and I was totally certain of where I was
going in life. I would finish my degree, go on to post-
graduate work, then head overseas to some adventurous
locale and start my career. I planned to date here and
there, but romance was no big deal. Just having fun.
After all, no woman was going to stand in the way of
Rick McKinley's plans! I had important things to accomplish. I pictured myself in the sweltering African heat,
wearing a big hat and helping children get clean water.
The next night I might be in a business suit, driving a
Beemer down the autobahn. I was not really driven
toward one particular goal, but I had dreams. And they
all involved *my* future and *my* relationship with *me*.

Then I met Jeanne and my world turned upside down.
I was so enamored with this girl that I was ready to lay
down my dreams and reimagine life. Why? Because this
new relationship had radically altered my heart, and I knew

it was going to radically alter the course of my life. And I welcomed it. I know some people would fight it; they might choose their career over a potential spouse. But I knew that Jeanne was made for me and I for her. Our relationship made me dream a different dream, and so I willingly reimagined life in light of this relationship of love.

This is just a small picture of what we've been talking about. Like my relationship with the woman who would become my wife, Jesus' invitation to leave the margins and join him in an intimate daily relationship requires that you start thinking differently about your future.

CHECKING THE MAIL

As I look back on my life, I can see now that Jesus was always there. I am blown away that even when I cut myself off from him, there he was, offering me love and acceptance and inviting me home. It's been an amazing journey out of the margins and learning to live in his grace. *Grace* is still something of a foreign word to me. I find myself trying to earn God's love from time to time, but then he reminds me: I can't earn it; I just have to receive it.

It's starting to make more and more sense to me that as I receive his love he calls me to give it away to other people. You see, not only does he love people like me, but he uses people like me to meet other people in *their* margins and begin to bring them out into the love of Jesus. And so I keep believing and obeying and reimagining life in his love. That is my goal for today.

I started the book by sharing with you a few post-cards from other people who were stuck in the margins. Let's check in with them and see what the view looks like further down the road.

Tiffany

I am always amazed at how God has met me in the deepest parts of me, parts I did not even know were there. When I first started dealing with the fact that I was sexually abused, I assumed that God couldn't care less about me. Now I realize that God has loved me the whole time. The abuse taught me that I was worthless, but Christ has taught me that I am precious to him.

The greatest thing is that in his love I could really forgive the person who hurt me and move on. Moving on is a daily thing for me. I can't say that it's cut-and-dried or that the pain is gone forever, but it is different now. I know how much God loves me, and I don't have to ignore the pain. I can go to my Father as his daughter and he will comfort me in that pain.

I am still single, but I don't give myself away to guys anymore. I see now that the love I was looking for can only be found in Jesus. I am a grateful daughter who is just trying to stay in my Father's love.

David

Coming to Jesus has been pretty wild. Since knowing him, I've realized some things that I'd kind of avoided before. I guess not having a dad was a pretty major deal for me. I stuffed it for most of my life, but the effects were there. For one thing, I wouldn't finish anything. I guess I was really scared of failing.

But accepting God as my Father has made a big impact on my life. Sometimes I still find myself wanting my real dad to have a relationship with me, but then I realize that's like telling God he is second best.

And I don't normally wake up feeling like I'm God's son. I lived with believing I was alone for so long, that's what comes natural to me. But when I take the time to really focus on what I believe, it all lines up. I might even go ahead and finish college. I just want to be able to say that I did it.

I'm still kind of a flake, but God is kicking my tail on that a bit. The truth is, I do feel accepted. I know God is there and he's happy to have me as his son. And that's pretty cool.

Jennifer

Now that Jesus is in my life I really see things differently. I used to think that if my parents had never gotten divorced then my life would have been perfect. I know now that is not the case. The thing I was really longing for was the

love and security of my heavenly Father, and it
has made all the difference. I don't cling to
thoughts of "what should have been" anymore.
Instead, I focus on what is and will be as I live in
the love of Jesus.

Christmas and family gatherings are weird
and can still dredge up the old pain. At those
times I am tempted to run back into the place
where I feel sorry for myself, but that's not where
life is for me. Now life is in Christ and his love and
knowing that the truest meaning of home is with
God in my heart. In that place I know I will not fall
apart and God is not going to leave. I am going to
keep believing and living in that love.

Peter

Jesus woke me up to some pretty tough things
in my life. I was trying to follow the world's
formula for success, and I almost lost my kids in
the process. I was running around after money
and things to make me happy, to give my life
meaning, when the whole time the really
important things were right in front of me.

When I gave myself to Jesus, I had to learn
what life was really all about. I wish I could say I
have it wired, but being a follower of Christ is not
as simple as closing a business deal. It's a
relationship and I closed off that part of me a
long time ago. Jesus didn't buy it though. He
gradually softened my heart until I was able to

ask my kids to forgive me for not being there for them. We have a ways to go in reestablishing a trusting relationship, but I am now able to engage them and let them know what they mean to me.

I wish I had met Jesus when I was younger; maybe things would have been different. But I have to trust that his timing is perfect. I really do believe that Jesus is the meaning of life that moves me to love and worship him above everything else. He knows me much better than I know myself, and I am learning to trust him with the big issues of my life. One step at a time, I am starting to get it. One thing for sure, I am not going back to where I was. This is too great to give up.

Liz

I had to come to grips with the fact that what I really wanted, more than Christ, was for people at my church to like me. Somewhere along the way, being liked became more important than loving people. I finally got up the courage to have an honest conversation with God about that, and I confessed it as a sin. Then I really sensed that Jesus was asking me to start some new friendships with people who don't yet believe in Jesus. It was scary at first. I didn't really know where to begin, but then God showed up.

I started volunteering to help with my son's soccer team, and I met three great ladies there. I had them over to dinner and started getting to know their stories. I was amazed to find out that they've all thought a lot about God and faith. I thought only people who go to church do that! My husband and I have started praying that God will open up ways for us to share with them what Jesus has done in our lives. We've had to explain to our kids what's going on, why they may hear a bad word now and then come from one the ladies or their husbands. One of the women smokes, so we've walked through that with our kids as well. I think they see that we really love these people and Jesus does, too.

I am a bit less involved at church and some of my friends there don't understand, but I won't go back to life in the bubble. Jesus is at work in these new friends' lives, and he is letting me be a part of their journey. They don't go to church and they haven't yet trusted Jesus with their lives, but I am leaving that up to God. I'm just glad to have the chance to tell them how much Jesus loves them.

DIANE, MY FRIEND

The story of Diane's journey came out in an earlier chapter. She passed away in October 2003, but her journals tell her story of how Jesus met her in the margins and she ended up reimagining life in his love. Even during her last year of life, as she suffered the physical devastation of Lou Gehrig's disease,

Diane's soul thrived. I want you to see what faith looks like—not just further down the road, but the kind of faith that takes you to the place of being in Jesus' presence.

In the early 1990s, she wrote about being in the margins:

> I want to have patience with myself. Please break the chains that destroy me, Lord. No more a victim, not even to myself. I want to choose freedom. Teach me to rest and to play and to delight in leaning on you. Lord, is there a way I can walk out of this? Is there a way I can learn to help others walk out of this? What does it look like? Where is my next step? I surrender to you, my loving Lord and Holy Master.

Many of us would get to watch Diane walk out of the margins. And God would use her to help others walk out of the margins. A journal entry from her last year shows the incredible love she was experiencing in Jesus:

> All day I have been reminded in tangible ways about your love and your love through others. Every aspect of my life, someone is helping me. It is evident that we are being lavished with your grace and mercy. I put our lives in your hands and trust that no place is a safer haven than in you. You know more than I will ever fathom. I remain in awe of you.

She would also journal what God was teaching her through the Bible and prayer:

"Be at peace my child, you are weary and your body is weak. Rest and love me with all your being. Diane, you are walking a path now that is so beyond you, but I will carry you. Trust me."

Diane did. And even in the face of death she lived honestly before God. Later she wrote:

Your ways be glorified, my God and Father. I lift my husband, daughters, sons-in-law, grandchildren, brothers, nieces, cousins, and family and friends up to YOU! Teach us how to walk in these days. We need you to hold us close and whisper in our ears, reminding us of your great faithfulness. Though my soul knows that dwelling eternally with you is right and good, I find myself torn in two emotion-ally not wanting to be physically removed from my dear, dear loved ones. Come into that place, I pray! I will trust you, my Father and Lord. Let your Holy Spirit show me and prompt me, I pray. Nothing is as I would imagine regarding how this would be for me.

As the months went by, Diane's condition wors-ened. She went from a walker to a wheelchair and yet continued in the love of Jesus:

Lord, my body seems to have many things
going wrong. Be my hope and strength. I am
weary tonight. I know you have not forgotten
me and so I dare to hope. I wait on you,
Father. Jesus, hold me that I may stand in
faith each day. I declare my hope in what is
not seen but is very, very real and incredibly
essential. God is the Creator and Father, Jesus
is my redeemer, and the Holy Spirit guides me
today.

As she grew weaker, the day I had dreaded came. I
had to talk to Diane about her funeral. She wrote of
this day:

The situation today requires decision. Rick
asked me who I would want to do my service,
and I told him I wanted him and Dave to do
it. As we talked, we both shed some tears.
Rick commented that it wouldn't be a funeral,
it would be a celebration. That I am sure of,
Lord! You have brought such depth, meaning,
and purpose to my life. For those things I am
eternally grateful to you. You have loved me
well. I have had an amazing life. I love the
family you created out of the chaos of my
childhood. Only YOU could do that. I have
trusted you and you have been faithful. The
day I dwell with you forever will be an incredible day for sure. I hope that the trusting,
the believing, the receiving, the caring, and

the outpouring of love are indicative of something to come. Your movement in your people
is profound. Your love, your compassion, your
dedication, your strength, your hope and
tenacity, and your unending promises are seen
in your people. I hope they are indicative of
things to come.

They *were* indicative of things to come. Diane
now stands face-to-face with the One who pulled her
out of the margins. The love she experienced through
the Spirit of God and the people of God was just a
small sample of the love she is experiencing right now
in the presence of Jesus.

Hers is a postcard from someone who is already
home. Jesus redeemed Diane to a life beyond measure,
and she walked in his love even through the valley of
the shadow of death. And Jesus proved faithful.

So many others have moved from the margins
into the love of Jesus. There is, as the Bible says, a
great cloud of witnesses who attest to the faithfulness
of Jesus. Will you trust him to take you out of the
margins? Will you, too, reimagine your life as one
who is saved and loved by Jesus?